EARLY PIETY ILLUSTRATED

EARLY PIETY ILLUSTRATED

*The Memoir of Nathan W. Dickerman,
The Little Sufferer Whose Testimony
Touched Hearts the World Over*

GORHAM ABBOTT

SOLID GROUND CHRISTIAN BOOKS
BIRMINGHAM, ALABAMA USA

Solid Ground Christian Books
2090 Columbiana Rd, Suite 2000
Birmingham, AL 35216
205-443-0311
sgcb@charter.net
http://solid-ground-books.com

Early Piety Illustrated
THE MEMOIR OF NATHAN W. DICKERMAN

Gorham Abbott

Taken from 1831 edition by Pierce & Parker, Boston, MA

Solid Ground Classic Reprints

First printing of new edition August 2005

Cover work by Borgo Design, Tuscaloosa, AL
Contact them at nelbrown@comcast.net

Cover image is a likeness of Nathan Dickerman which was sketched by a
portrait artist of that day named Mr. Edwards. See page 92 of this book.

ISBN: 1-59925-012-8

Preface to New Edition

"A little child shall lead them."

The little book you hold in your hand is a beautiful illustration of the above text from Isaiah 11:6. The little child the Lord raised up nearly two hundred years ago was Nathan W. Dickerman, and the following pages tell his story in the words of those who knew him in a deeply personal way.

Let me warn you that you will find yourself again and again questioning the possibility of a seven year old thinking and speaking the way Nathan does. The fact is, his case was so unusual in *that* day that it was felt necessary to include letters of commendation from his pastors and parents, which will be found on the following few pages.

Be prepared for lessons of life from a young boy on his death bed, in the last stages of a painful disease that made his every breath a burden. Be prepared for a sight of the grace of God at work in the frail body of a seven year old. Be prepared to be encouraged, comforted, convicted and blessed as you enter into a sick room where hundreds of people went to "see for themselves" the little boy who became the talk of Boston.

It has been a genuine delight for me to sit at the feet of young Nathan and learn from him. I have been shown once again a moving illustration of our Lord's words: *"My power is made perfect in weakness"* (2 Corinthians 12:9), and of the words of the Apostle Paul: *"God has chosen the weak things of the world to confound the things that are mighty"* (1 Corinthians 1:27).

May you find the words of Nathan, his pastors, his friends, the hymns and portions of Sacred Scripture to be heaven-sent, as you face whatever challenges the Lord has sent your way.

Michael Gaydosh, the editor
Labor Day 2005

The following Memoir was submitted in manuscript to the perusal of the Rev. Drs. William Jenks and B.B. Wisner of Boston. Dr. Jenks returned it accompanied with the letter that follows. Dr. Wisner has added his own testimonial to the correctness of the representations. Finally, the parents of Nathan have also read the narrative twice in the course of its preparation, and have given it their sanction.

Dr. William Jenks's Letter

Boston, Sept. 21, 1830

My Dear Sir,

I have perused with a deep interest, as you may well imagine, your *Memorial of Nathan Dickerman*. It has convinced me that I had judged well in urging the task upon *you*, instead of attempting, as I was repeatedly requested, to do it myself. Your assiduous attention, the frequency of your visits, your practice of reducing to writing the results of your repeated observation—while it was impracticable for me to hear and understand, on all occasions, the remarks made when I was present, and out of my power to spend with the child so much time as would, for such a purpose, be demanded—all these considerations strengthen my conviction.

What I have read is now, so far as my knowledge extends, and recollection serves me, a plain, unvarnished statement of matters of fact. I have little to add to the detail—which, I am somewhat fearful, may be judged, by some, too minute;—but it still seems expedient that I should add a little, in order to make a few things more clear.

The dear boy was not originally a member of my flock, and was hence totally unknown to me, till his sickness, and subsequent expression of religious hope, had rendered him an object of peculiar attention to two of the brethren of the Church under my care, Mr. H. and Mr. B. These Christian brethren were teachers in the Sabbath School. At their request I visited Nathan, about the time that his desire to be admitted to the Church appears in your Narrative.

You may well suppose that the expression of such a desire, by one so young, would excite deliberation and inquiry. No example had occurred in the city, of so early an admission to the privileges of the Church. And yet these privileges were pleaded for in terms so scriptural, and under circumstances so interesting, that it seemed inexpedient, and even cruel, to withhold them. "If I have received the Spirit, as Christians tell me they think I have," argued the dear child, as was reported to me, "then, why should I not profess his name?" Accordingly, measures were taken by us for his regular admission to the Church, and due enjoyment of its privileges.

I visited him often, yet, probably, not so often as he desired. He ever received me with the most grateful affection and respect; and I think I never was with him without being requested to pray, if I had not myself first suggested it. In the very first conversation, upon being asked, "What made you first think of Christ and of your soul?"—his reply speaks a volume of encouragement to the benevolent instructors of the young in our Sabbath Schools: "My teacher, sir." Yes, the teacher is happy, who was God's instrument in feeding this lamb of the flock of Christ.

During the period since I entered the pulpit, which is now about three and thirty years, I have never seen so bright and sweet an exhibition of early and efficient piety. His religion was not a display of mere affection, uttering itself in the fond expressions which have disgusted the judicious in some books of devotion, as savoring too much of mere earthly love and presuming familiarity; it was a strong attachment, as intellectual as it could well be in such a subject, reverential, holy, devout, and yet, in a very remarkable degree, if not thoroughly, *practical.* No sooner had he obtained a standing for himself on the tenable ground of a Christian hope, than he was desirous of drawing all around him toward the same safe position. His father, mother, sisters, relations, schoolfellows, play-mates, and acquaintances, were all encircled in the arms of his tender, Christ-like benevolence. This appears so fully in your Narrative, that I hardly need to exemplify it further. It beams, however, most radiantly, perhaps, in the remarkable business-transaction of the pew.[a] And I am happy to say, that from the time of Nathan's death to the present, that pew has been occupied by the family. More than this, his dear, afflicted mother has been led to

---

[a] The account of this transaction is recorded on page 93.

profess her subjection to the faith of the Gospel, and is now a member of the same Church to which her beloved son was joined.

My own little son, who was separated from us by death, in somewhat more than three months after Nathan's departure, was deeply interested in him. This fact I mention, specially, to show the impression made on other young minds by his character: "Papa," said my son to me one day, during his own sickness, "I suppose Nathan Dickerman loves God so much, that he doesn't wish to get well, but had rather die and go to God." Such was the judgment formed of him by one nearly a year younger. What effect it had, we are not permitted to know—but it could have been no otherwise, it would seem, than salutary.

As you have related, I was present on the morning of Nathan's death. Mr. B. came to inform me that an alteration had evidently occurred the preceding night; yet stated that it was feared Nathan was not fully sensible how near his departure might be. His mother, therefore, wished me to communicate it to him. I need not say how delicate the task seemed to be, and yet how necessary. But I found him so prepared for the intelligence, that it gave him, apparently, no shock whatever.

I was not present at the funeral, being detained that day by the peculiarly critical situation of my own son. But it was a day of deep interest at Braintree; and I cannot but hope and expect, that impressions then made, under not only the solemnities of the scene itself, but the administrations of Rev. Messrs. Storrs and Perkins also, will be found of eternal benefit to souls not a few.

Hoping and praying that the Great Head of the Church will render your labor useful to the rising generation, and instrumental in the salvation of very many souls,

I am, my dear sir,
Respectfully and affectionately,
Yours,   WM. JENKS

Dr. B.B. Wisner's Letter

I am well acquainted with the writer of the following Narrative, and with nearly all the persons from whose accounts of their visits to the subject of it the work has been chiefly compiled. During Nathan's sickness, I visited him twice, and often conversed with others who saw him more frequently. I have read the whole of the Narrative in manuscript, and I have no hesitation in saying that it is an unvarnished account of real facts.

B. B. WISNER
Boston, Sept. 24, 1830

Nathan's Parent's Letter

We take pleasure in stating that we have been well acquainted, during the past year, with the compiler of this memoir of our son. He was accustomed to call almost every day, and sometimes more frequently, to see Nathan during the last few months of his sickness. The memoir we have read, and it is correct according to our best recollection; and it meets our approbation in every respect.

NATHAN DICKERMAN
REBECCA A. DICKERMAN
Boston, Sept. 29, 1830

Table of Contents

CHAPTER ONE

Nathan's father and mother. His character when a little boy. Goes to Sabbath School. Anecdotes. His interest in religion. He is sick, and goes to visit his grandmother in the country. More anecdotes. What he thought of bad boys on the Common. He returns to Boston. His love for his physician, Dr. Gorham. Dr. Gorham's death, and Nathan's sorrow. Nathan is very sick, and is much afraid that he shall die.

NATHAN W. DICKERMAN was born in Boston, Massachusetts, on March 26, 1822. He died in the same city, January 2, 1830. He had two sisters,—Maria, a little older, and Rebecca, a few years younger than himself.

Mr. and Mrs. Dickerman had always lived in Boston, and little Nathan, their son, spent almost all his days in that city. He was a pleasant boy. When quite young, he was very lively and playful. He was very fond of his parents. It gave him great pleasure to go with his father when he went upon his business; and as he was an only son, it was very natural for his father to love him very much.

At an early age, his parents placed him at school, and he there became so good a scholar,[1] and was generally so attentive and diligent in his studies, that he was not only beloved by his instructress, but was esteemed by all who knew him. His manners, too, were so becoming, and he was so affectionate in his behavior towards his playmates, that he was loved of all the boys in school.

---

[1] A 'scholar' was a term used in a more general sense in the nineteenth century, and would be used as we would use the word pupil or student.

1

Nathan in his earlier years received but little religious instruction. He and his sisters were only taught by their mother to say their prayers, to speak the truth, and to use no wicked words.

Although Nathan was a pleasant boy, and a good scholar, and amiable in his disposition and manners, like a great many other amiable children and good scholars, he often said and did what was wrong. But as he had been taught that it was wicked and vulgar to speak falsehood, or to use bad language, he was not often found guilty of such shameful conduct. Yet it appears, from what he once said to his grandmamma, that he sometimes committed even these great sins. However, he was generally very careful about falling into such wicked practices, which other people, as well as God, would see; and some persons supposed that he was an uncommonly good little boy.

But his parents, as much as they loved him, think he was like other children,—sometimes obedient to them, true to his word, diligent and faithful, mild and affectionate with his sisters and associates—and sometimes not so.

Little Nathan had many friends who loved him very much, and who remember well, now, although he is dead, how he studied his book at school—and played at home—and did errands for his parents. But especially his teachers and friends at the Sabbath School, remember his attentive appearance there; and those who had the privilege of visiting his sick chamber and his dying bed, delight to remember how patient he was when suffering, and how happy when expecting to die and go to heaven, and to think upon many things which he said, when they were with him.

Of Nathan's thoughts and feelings about religion, before he was five years old, we know very little. He doubtless lived and felt like most boys of his age, who are exposed to the bad influence of others at school, and meet many temptations in the streets to do wrong.

When he was about five years old, a gentleman, interested in the Hawkins Street Sabbath School, called upon his mother,

2

and requested her to send her son. The parents cheerfully accepted the invitation, and the next Sabbath, Nathan, for the first time in his life, was a Sabbath School scholar.

Previous to this time, he had never attended church on the Sabbath, or any other religious meeting, and we have no reason to think he ever said or thought much about religion.

But the instruction which he now began to receive from his Sabbath School teacher awakened his attention. He became deeply interested in what he heard and learned. His mind was so much occupied in thinking about it, that he appeared differently at home during the week, so that his parents and the neighbors noticed the change.

A remark which he made to his mother one day, after returning from school, strikingly illustrates this. The superintendent had addressed the scholars on the necessity of a new heart, in order to please God, and be happy. Nathan, after giving at home an account of the address, added, "and I am sure, mamma, he meant *me*, for he looked right at me."

His fondness for the Sabbath School, and his attachment to the teachers often appeared during the week. If at any time he met in the street the superintendent, or any teacher, he seemed very happy to see him, made his bow and spoke to him, and afterwards told at home, whom he had seen. Often since his death, have different teachers alluded to the pleasant smile with which little Nathan greeted them, whenever they chanced to meet him, out of school.

Soon after having entered the Sabbath School, he began to go to Dr. Jenks's meeting, and was there very attentive to the preaching and the prayers. He discovered the same affection for his minister, that he did for his teacher, and in the same way, always telling with great delight at home, if he had met him in the street.

He was very careful to remember the instruction he received on the Sabbath, either at meeting or at school, and used often to repeat at home, not only the texts, but what was said by the minister, or by his teacher or superintendent. Sometimes he has, in a most affectionate manner reproved those at home, who said or did anything which was wrong; and when asked how he knew it was wicked has said, "The minister said so," or, "my teacher said so," or, "the Bible says so."

He used to stop on communion Sabbaths, and on such occasions, was much interested in the exercises; and also in baptisms, and the admission of members to the church.

It is very evident, that his interest in religious truth was gradually increasing, although no permanent impression seemed to be made on his mind until after several months. An incident, which occurred when he had been three or four months at school, shows clearly how strong an influence truth was gaining over him.

One Sabbath, Mr. D., the superintendent in his address to the school, spoke of the duty of secret prayer, and urged upon all to begin immediately to kneel before God, and pray, in their bed-chambers, morning and evening. When Nathan came home, he told the family that they all ought to pray; and the next morning, as he slept in the same room with his parents, he rose early, and went to his mother's bedside. He touched her elbow. She awoke and found him standing in tears. She said to him,

"What do you want, Nathan?"

"Mamma," said he, "where shall I kneel?"

"What for, Nathan?" said she.

"To pray, mamma, for a new heart," he replied.

Another little anecdote shows the bent of his mind. About this time, while going on an errand for his school-mistress, he was caught out in a violent storm of wind and rain. It was so severe, that he had some difficulty in getting safely home. He succeeded, however, although pretty thoroughly drenched in the shower, and almost out of breath.

His mother asked him where he had been.

"I've been on an errand, mamma," said he; "and I'll tell you what I thought.—I was thinking, that God sent that wind and rain upon me, because I was so wicked."

"*Why,* Nathan?" said she.

4

"Because I was so wicked, mamma," he repeated.

At another time, he slipped away from his mother, and she did not notice his absence immediately. She soon, however, had occasion to call for him, and did so several times. In a few minutes he came from some secret place, out of her sight. She said, "Where have you been, Nathan!—I have been calling for you, sometime."

"I have been praying, mamma," said he, "for a new heart; and I prayed for you, too, mamma."

He was sometimes laughed at, for his seriousness, and his religious remarks, but he never seemed, in the least degree, irritated or angry, though he often burst into tears, and afterwards said to others, he should pray for those who laughed at him.

About this time, he came into the house one day, having left a company of boys in the street, and said, "Mamma, I sha'nt play with those bad boys any more, they speak such bad words."

Nathan began to go to the Sabbath School, in March 1827, when he was just five years old. He continued to attend until July, 1828, a little more than a year,—by which time he was six years and four months old. And it was during this year that what is related above occurred.

But he was now taken sick. An inflammation in his chest occasioned so severe an illness as to deprive him, for several months, of the privilege of attending public worship and the Sabbath School. During this time, while confined at home, he often displayed considerable seriousness. His mother remembers that he very frequently asked her to read in the Bible to him and talk with him. She once asked him, "What shall I talk about, Nathan?"

"About Heaven, mamma," he replied.

After he had been sick three or four months, he went, in Oct. 1829, to spend a few weeks with his grandmother at Braintree; his friends hoping that a ride in the country would benefit his health.

His grandmother describes his appearance, while with her, as quite serious, and in every respect becoming. He often made remarks upon religious subjects, but they never attracted her attention particularly, until one day, when the following incident occurred.

He was sitting with his grandmother and aunt at the dinner table, and when they had finished their meal, Nathan said, "Now grandmamma, let us all rise from the table together."

"What for, Nathan?" said she. "To pray over the table, grandmamma,—all good people do."

While in the country, he was able sometimes to go a visiting. One day, after he had returned from a visit to one of his aunts, he was asked what his aunt said to him.

"She said," he replied—"I *believe* she said, I must come and see her again, but I don't remember for certain; that isn't telling a lie, is it grandmamma?" When his grandmother had answered the question, he waited a little, very thoughtfully, and then said, "How many of the boys tell lies and say wicked words. It's a great while grandmamma, since I said any, and I don't remember when I told a lie."

One evening, he had been sitting by the side of his grandmother, at the window, when she left him for a few moments. On returning to her seat, she found him on his knees in the corner. She was much surprised, and she waited sometime in silence after he arose, wishing him to speak first, that she might know what he would say of his own accord. But at length, as she expected some one would come in and interrupt them, she asked what he had been doing.

"I have been praying," said he, "for a new heart, grandmamma,—do you think I shall have it?"

At another time, as she was conversing with him about prayer, she asked what he prayed for.

He told her, he prayed, "that his sins might be forgiven, and for his parents."

6

He was very anxious to go to meeting while at Braintree. But as he went away from home rather unexpectedly, and it was uncertain how long he would be absent, his mother did not send his Sabbath-day suit of clothes; and his grandmother told him that she thought his clothes were not suitable, and that his mother would be unwilling to have him appear at meeting so. But she could not prevail upon him, on account, to stay away. He said, "Well, grandmamma, I'll put on my great coat, and wrap it tight around my pantaloons, and nobody will know it."

The kind, affectionate, yet earnest manner in which he sometimes tried to persuade others to attend worship, would seem to be almost irresistible. He said, one Sabbath,

"Now, grandpapa, you *will* go to meeting today, won't you? You'll go this afternoon, won't you, grandpapa?"

He was very much grieved when he heard or saw anything that was wicked. He was once found weeping bitterly, after something of this kind had occurred, and being asked what made him cry, he answered,

"They are so wicked, and God keeps a book of remembrance."

When he saw any word denoting a spiritual object, he would say, "O, grandmamma, what a *good* word that is." One day he came into the house, and said, "Grandmamma, I can't bear to hear the boys speak such bad words; it makes me shiver—it makes me think of the wicked people on the Common."[2]

He was once in a situation where he expected a person would come home in the evening that used profane language. And he asked to be put to bed before the person came, that he might not hear wicked words.

---

[2] Children in the country, perhaps, do not know that on the 4th of July, and on Election days, and other public occasions, Boston Common, a large and beautiful green, almost surrounded by trees, is covered with thousands of people, who come together for amusement, and Nathan knew that many of them were very wicked and very profane.

Nathan returned to his parents at Boston on a Saturday, about the last of November, much better than when he went away. He was very much pleased and benefited by the religious conversation and advice of his grandmother. His mother distinctly remembers his pleasant countenance and smile, as he came into the house, on his return, and ran to her arms, very glad indeed to see her, but he said, "Mamma, I'm only come home to see you, and stay a little while, and then I'm going back to stay with grandmamma; mayn't I, mamma?" Afterwards, when he became very sick in Boston, he wanted to have his grandmother to come in and see him. And when she was expected, he often said, "Oh! how I *long* to see grandmamma. What *good* meetings we will have."

The very next day he was in his class at the Sabbath School again, and his looks showed how happy he was to be there.

He seemed almost every week to be more and more interested in what he was taught. His parents and friends noticed the change in his appearance more distinctly than ever before. One day he said to his mother,

"Mamma, I wonder why I cannot pray as they do at the Sabbath School? I can only say, 'Our Father.' He then asked, "Mamma, if I should say besides that, Lord Jesus give me a new heart,—would that be praying?"

Many other interesting incidents occurred during this second period of his attending the Sabbath School, which are not remembered now. He continued to attend regularly and punctually every week, till the first Sabbath in January, 1829, which was the last day he ever went. He was now not quite seven years old, and the inflammation in his chest returned and settled upon his heart. He was confined to the house most of the time until May, when his physician allowed him to be sent again, to spend a few weeks with his grandmother. But his disease grew worse, and he returned home about the first of July. After this, he went out of the house but very little, if at all. He pined away gradually, until he died, January 2nd, 1830.

Dr. Gorham attended him until his own death. But afterwards, he received visits from many other eminent physicians. No one conversed with him, personally, on the subject of religion, until after Dr. Gorham's death.

He was very strongly attached to Dr. Gorham. He seemed to love him, almost as a parent, and used to count the number of his visits.

When it was told him that Dr. G. was dead, Nathan burst into tears and exclaimed, "Oh, I hope he has gone to heaven." Soon afterwards he almost fainted; so that they were obliged to apply cordials in order to revive him.

After this, his anxiety about his own salvation was much increased. Previously on one occasion his grandmother made known to him her fears about his recovery, and asked him if he thought he should get well again.

He replied, crying, "I don't know; sometimes I think I shall, and sometimes I think I sha'nt."

He now became very deeply engaged in religious subjects, was very desirous of having his teachers come and pray with him, and *very often* requested his mother to read the Bible and talk to him.

Not infrequently has she found him in tears, and on inquiring into the cause, he has answered to this effect:

"I don't think I shall ever get well, and I want a new heart."—"I shouldn't fear to die, if I thought I could go to that good place."

At this time, he manifested great fear of death. And in conversation on the subject, he sometimes became so agitated that it was with no little difficulty they could calm his feelings.

When, however, he found "hope and peace in believing," he was accustomed to say, "I have no fear of death now,"— "Death has no terrors for me now."

CHAPTER TWO

Many persons visit Nathan. Journals and Memoranda. Mr. Shedd. The Author's first visit. Various anecdotes. He wishes to be baptized. He talks about it with his Grandmother, his Mother, and Dr. Jenks. The hymns which he liked to hear.

My young readers have read in the last chapter, the account of little Nathan's life, up to the first of July, 1829, which was six months before he died. He was at that time only a little more than seven years old.

Almost all that remains to be told about this good little boy relates to what took place during these last six months. In this time a great many people visited him and conversed with him, and have remembered what he said.

Among those who were most interested in Nathan, and who for a time visited him most frequently, was the Rev. Mr. Shedd[3] of Abington, Mass. Abington is a town not far from Braintree, and Mr. Shedd became acquainted with the little sufferer there, and continued his acquaintance, and his visits after the boy returned to Boston.

Nathan became very much attached to this minister, and it was intended that this Memoir should have been prepared by him. All the papers and memoranda were, after Nathan's death, put into Mr. Shedd's hands for this purpose. He commenced the

---

[3] This was Dr. William Shedd (1798-1830), not to be confused with W.G.T. Shedd (1820-1894), whose writings continue to bless the Church of Christ.

work; but in a very few days he was taken sick; and obliged to lay aside the labor. He hoped soon to be able to resume it; but he was disappointed. His health was not restored. He lingered many months in sickness and pain and then sank into the grave.

Some persons wrote down afterwards what they saw and heard in his sick chamber. Some kept a kind of journal, or regular account of visits which they made him, writing every day, immediately after they saw him, how he appeared. I have now before me various writings of this kind, which have been received from different individuals. They are Letters, Journals, Memoranda, &c., which I shall transcribe, as nearly as possible, in the order of time in which they are dated.

The first is the journal of the writer of these pages, who visited him, regularly, with few interruptions almost every day, from the last of September, until within a fortnight[4] of his death. He had been making visits to Nathan, a short time before he commenced his journal. This explains those cases, where Nathan refers to a previous interview or conversation, of which no record is made.

The journal begins as follows:

Sept. 29, 1829. A short time ago, a lady invited me to call with her and visit a little boy, who was said to be very sick. He is about seven years old. Soon after I went in today, he began to talk about the Sabbath School, and asked me whenever I should see any scholars, to talk with them about the Savior. I asked him what he thought was the best way to talk with others;—to tell them of their sins, and of their dreadful danger as sinners, while they refuse to repent,—or to tell them of the love of the Savior, and of what He had suffered in their place, that they might be forgiven?

He replied—"I should like to tell them both."

He said something about Sabbath School books, and I named several to him that were particularly interesting, and appropriate to his case. I mentioned also a little tract, which I

---

[4] A fortnight is fourteen days.

thought would please him; it was called—'Lead me to the Rock, that is higher than I,' and I asked him, if he knew what that text meant. He hesitated a moment and then replied,

"Yes sir, I think I do."

"What do you think it means?"

"Jesus Christ," he answered.

Once today, Nathan was left alone, with his mother, and the following conversation, as related by her to me, took place between them. He had been looking towards his mother with much affection for sometime, and then asked,

"Mamma, if I die, shall you cry?"

His mother, surprised at the question, hardly knew what to say, but at length replied, "I don't know—why, Nathan?"

"I shouldn't like to have you cry," said he; "and I shouldn't think you would, when I am going to a better world. Mamma, why can't you be good?"

"I don't know Nathan,"—she replied, "I can't."

'Why yes, mamma, you can; only repent, and believe in the Lord Jesus Christ."

Oct. 3. Found Nathan, this evening, more comfortable. Soon after I went in, he asked his mother to get the Bible, and wished me to read a chapter to him. I inquired if there was any particular part he would like. His mother replied that since my last visit he had selected a chapter for me to read when I should come again.

When his mother had brought the Bible, Nathan took it before him, as he sat up in the bed, and holding it in his lap, turned over the pages to the 116th Psalm, beginning,

"I love the Lord, because he hath heard my voice and my supplications."

He read over aloud and slowly the first verse and then handed the book to me.

When I had read the third verse, *"The sorrows of death compassed me, and the pains of hell gat hold upon me; I found trouble and sorrow,"* I made some remark, on the dreadful sorrow and trouble of those who refuse to repent while they have life and health, and come to a death bed unprepared. He interrupted me, saying, "I heard of a man who died lately,—he died dreadfully; he was a wicked man,—and made a mock of religion,—and when he died, he shrieked dreadfully."

And while I was reading one of the following verses, he spoke again of his own accord, saying,

"When I think of the people, who will not come to God, it makes me feel dreadfully,—it seems as though I could cry, almost."

Oct. 4. Sabbath Evening. Went to see Nathan.

He had been quite free from bodily suffering during the day. I asked him, if he had felt happy.

"Yes sir," said he, "but I have had some wicked thoughts."

Presently, in the course of conversation, I asked if he had been distressed with fear that he was not prepared to die.

"Yes sir," he replied, "sometimes I have,—and I wanted to talk with somebody, to know whether I *was* prepared."

Pretty soon, one of his little sisters came into the room, and while I was talking a few moments with her, I could hear him, as he lay on the pillow with his eyes closed, repeating to himself, several times over, in a low whisper,

'Begone unbelief, my Savior is near;'
'Begone unbelief, my Savior is near.'[5]

Before I left him, he asked to have prayers. I read the account of Paul and Silas, in the 16th chapter of the Acts. While reading, he would now and then make a remark, showing that he had read the chapter before.

As I attempted to explain how it was, that they while bound in prison, could sing praises to God,—and how all that really love the Savior can be happy, even in affliction and severe bodily suffering, his countenance lighted up, as if he could bear witness, that

---

[5] This hymn was written by John Newton.

—'they whose hearts
Are stayed on God, are kept *in peace,*
Though troubles rise.'

When I had finished the chapter, he said,

"Don't you think that the jailor and the family must have felt dreadfully, when they first saw themselves sinners?"

Before prayer he opened the Village Hymn Book, to find a hymn to be read, and spoke of two, which had given him "a great deal of comfort."

'Begone, unbelief,
My Savior is near;
And for my relief,
Will surely appear.'

And,

'T'is a point I long to know,
Oft it causes anxious thought,
Do I love the Lord or no,
Am I his, or am I not?'[6]

Oct. 14. Nathan was much more feeble today than I have ever seen him. He was very pale, excepting a little spot of hectic[7] on his cheek. His limbs had been very painful all day, and his feet, particularly, were swollen, as in the last stages of consumption. He was, however, perfectly pleasant and mild, although too sick to be cheerful. He was unable to talk much, but said, with very great interest, soon after I entered:—

"Dr. Jenks has been to see me today, and perhaps he will come and baptize me,"

I asked him, if he had been happy, when suffering so much pain.

"Pretty comfortable," he replied; "it seemed to me that my Savior was near."

---

[6] This hymn was written by John Newton.

[7] A feverish mark related to the disease of consumption, or tuberculosis.

"What do you love to think about most," said I, "when you are in pain?"

"The Lord Jesus Christ," he answered.

Soon after, as I was looking silently at the sweet expression of his countenance, admiring the lovely image of piety and peace, he looked up with a gentle, pensive look, and drawing a long breath, almost with a sigh, and evidently in pain, said,

"Oh! I long for heaven."

It was not often that Nathan was able to engage in a connected conversation. The influence of disease was such as to prevent the close attention of his mind to any subject for any length of time.

Sometimes, however, I tried to converse with him, and confine the conversation to some particular subject, in order to see whether his views were clear and distinct. One day I went to see him, wishing to ascertain what he thought about sin. The following conversation took place.

"Have you ever thought, Nathan, how long you might expect to live?"

He did not seem very ready to answer, and I could not understand what he said.

"Well, Nathan, should you feel willing to go tonight, if it were God's will?"

"Yes sir."

"Do you ever feel any anxiety, lest you should be deceived and think you were prepared to die, when you were not?"

"Yes sir, sometimes I do; and I feel as though I should like to know, whether I was ready—whether I was going to heaven or not."

"Well, I should like to have you tell me what your feelings were, when you first thought of the subject, and what first led you to think of it."

"My teacher told me about *the goodness of heaven*, and I thought I never could go there—for he said, we must be prepared, or go into everlasting punishment."

16

"What made you think that you could not go to heaven?"

"Because I was wicked."

"How did you know you was wicked?"

"They told me I had a wicked heart, and that it must be changed."

"Did you think you was wicked, for any other reason than because they *told* you so?"

"Yes sir, I *felt* that I had a wicked heart."

"And what did you do, when you *felt* this?"

"I prayed for a new heart."

"And do you know, Nathan, how long it was, after you began to think you was a sinner, and prayed for a new heart, before you hoped that God had answered your prayers?"

He hesitated.

"Perhaps you do not remember," I added.

"No sir, I don't," he replied.

"Do you remember what first led you to hope that God had given you a new heart?"

"No sir."[8]

At another time, I asked him, in conversation on the same subject, how a little boy might commit sin.

"He might swear and steal, and other things," said he.

"But suppose he does not *do* anything wrong, can he sin in any other way?"

"Yes sir, in wicked thoughts and words," he replied.

Oct. 15. Thursday Evening, 8. Called three-quarters of an hour since, upon Nathan, and found him asleep. His mother thought he had had a pretty comfortable day; but only a few moments after I entered he appeared very restless and uneasy, as he lay upon his pillow. He suddenly started up,—apparently still in his sleep, and then laid himself down again. His mother

---

[8] Once when his grandmother asked him a similar question, he said, 'I was praying, grandmamma, and while I prayed I was happy; and I have been happy ever since.'

17

went immediately to his bedside, and as she bent down over him, he burst into tears, and cried out most bitterly. We were quite alarmed at this; for he had never been known to appear so agitated, at any time, however severely he might be suffering. Mrs. Dickerman tried to compose him, and he soon became calm and easy.

I said, "Put your trust in the Savior, Nathan. He will be a very present help in every time of need."

"Yes sir," he replied immediately, smiling through his tears.

He then raised his arm gently around his mother's neck, and said, "Please to rock me;" and when rocking in her arms, looked sweetly at me and said, "Will you please to read a passage to me?"

I read the account of our Savior's suffering in the garden, as related by three of the Evangelists, comparing the accounts together. When I came to the verse in Matthew 26,—'*My soul is exceeding sorrowful, even, unto death,*' he whispered, in a low, still tone, each word before I pronounced it. '*My—soul—is—exceeding—sorrowful—even—unto—death.*'

And when the verse in the 22nd of Luke was read,—'*Nevertheless, not my will, but thine be done,*' he said,

"Yes sir, I often say that to myself."

After he had listened to the next verse, '*And there appeared an angel from Heaven strengthening him,*' He was reminded that there were many promises of assistance from above, *to us,* in the hour of affliction.

"Yes sir," said he, "I know it.—The Bible says afflictions are needful—and it is good *for me* that I have been afflicted;—it is needful for us; but God will sanctify it—to some people—to those that love the Savior."

Afterwards, while I was looking at him and watching the struggle which he made to keep quiet, in his severe pain, he turned to me, and said,

"Oh! how we ought to praise the Lord, that there are Sabbath Schools,—and the Bible, and a Savior. Mr. P. was the first one who asked mamma to let *me* go to the Sabbath

School.—Oh! Mr. Abbott, Dr. Jenks is going to let me know whether he will come and baptize me, and if you will come in this evening, I will let you know."

He had often spoken with the greatest interest of his being baptized, both when alone with his mother, and when others were present. His grandmother came into the city, about this time, to see him. He named the subject to her, and asked her questions about it. During their conversation she asked what first made him think of being baptized.

He replied, "Why I saw it in the New Testament, grandmamma."

It will, however, be remembered, that he witnessed this ordinance often, at church, after he began to attend public worship.

One day, as he was asking his mother, if she was willing that he should be baptized, she replied, "I think you had better not say anything more about it, Nathan. You are so young, I don't think it would be proper."

"But, mamma," said he, looking up into her face, "Jesus said, *'Suffer little children to come unto me, and forbid them not; for of such is the kingdom of Heaven.'*"[9]

He was very careful and desirous to obtain his parents' consent and approbation, in all that he wanted; and, at another time, as he was rocking in his mother's arms, while they were alone, he asked her again if she was willing. She tried to dissuade him from it, and said to him, in substance, as follows:

"Now, Nathan, hadn't you better give up the idea of being baptized, and not think any more about it? You may perhaps get well, yet, and if you should, and should go to school again, the boys might laugh at you; and shouldn't you feel ashamed then?" He instantly replied,

"Oh! no, mamma, if I should be ashamed of Jesus, when I come to die he will be ashamed of me."

---

[9] Mark 10:14.

And after thinking in silence a moment, he added, before his mother spoke again,

> 'Ashamed of Jesus! that dear friend
> On whom my hopes of heaven depend!
> No! when I blush, be this my shame:
> That I no more revere his name.'[10]

At another time, just after this conversation, a gentleman, Mr. H., was reading to him the account of the Eunuch's baptism in the 8th chapter of Acts. When he had read the 37th verse,
'And Philip said, "If thou believest with all thine heart, thou mayest." And he answered and said," I believe that Jesus Christ is the Son of God."

Nathan turned to his mother and said, "Well, mamma, just so I believe, and why can't I be baptized?"

On another occasion, a person conversing with him, offered some objection to his being baptized; and he answered one of the remarks, saying, "Why, *I believe in the Lord Jesus Christ, and why can't I be?"*

Dr. Jenks, writing on this subject, says as follows:
You may well suppose that the expression of such a desire, by one so young, would excite deliberation and inquiry. No example had occurred in the city, of so early an admission to the privileges of the church. And yet these privileges were pleaded for in terms so scriptural, and under circumstances so interesting, that it seemed inexpedient, and even cruel to withhold them. "If I have received the Spirit, as Christians tell me they think I have," argued the dear child, as was reported to me, "then *what doth hinder me to be baptized?"'* Accordingly, measures were taken by us, for his regular admission to the Church, and due enjoyment of its privileges.

Oct. 19. *Monday Evening.* Nathan is very sick tonight. His heart is beating most violently and rapidly, while the pulse can hardly

---

[10] Hymn written by Joseph Grigg.

be perceived at the wrist. But he says he is more happy than usual. I asked him why. He replied, "Because my Savior is nearer."

"Well, Nathan," said I, "it seems as though you were near to your home; your pains must be nearly ended, and how does Heaven appear to you now?"

He replied with a lovely smile, "Blessed."

After exchanging a few words with him, he said, "Oh, I have learned these two hymns—

> 'One there is above all others
> Well deserves the name of Friend,'[11]

And,

> 'The day is past and gone,
> The evening shades appear.'[12]

I had sometime before carried in to him Nettleton's Village Hymn Book,[13] with which he seemed very much pleased. Some of the hymns he committed to memory, and sometimes took great pleasure in repeating them. The two just named were particular favorites, as will be seen hereafter.

This hymn book has been shown to many Sabbath Schools since Nathan's death. The marks which he put in, and the pages turned down, at his favorite hymns, are still preserved as Nathan left them.

Oct. 21. Found him, this day-noon, suffering from a very severe headache, and a white handkerchief was bound tightly around his forehead, to alleviate, if possible, the great pain; he looked however, as smiling and happy as usual. I asked him how he felt.

"Rather easier," said he.

---

[11] This hymn is by John Newton (see p. 25 for complete hymn).

[12] This hymn was written by John Leland (see pp. 23,24 for complete hymn).

[13] Asahel Nettleton (1783-1844) was a leading figure in the Second Great Awakening in America. His Village Hymn Book was very popular.

Presently he said, "Mamma, will you take me up," and while she was removing him from the bed to the rocking chair, he underwent, apparently, the most intense suffering, but bore it all with the greatest patience.

His cough was so violent, that he could not say much, but soon asked for the hymn book and desired the hymn to be read.

'Jesus at thy command,
I launch into the deep,
And leave my native land,
Where sin lulls all asleep;
For Thee, I fain would all resign,
And sail to heaven with Thee and Thine.

Thou art my Pilot wise;
My compass is thy word;
My soul each storm defies,
While I have such a Lord !
I trust Thy faithfulness and power,
To save me in the trying hour.

Though rocks and quick-sands deep,
Through all my passage lie;
Yet thou wilt safely keep,
And guide me with thine eye:
My anchor, hope, shall firm abide,
And I each boisterous storm outride.

By faith, I see the land,
The port of endless rest;
My soul, thy sails expand,
And fly to Jesus' breast,
Oh ! may I reach the heavenly shore,
Where winds and waves distress no more.

Whene'er becalmed I lie,
And storms and winds subside;
Lord, to my succor fly,
And keep me near thy side;
For more the treacherous calm I dread.
Than tempests bursting o'er my head.

Come, heavenly wind, and blow,
A prosperous gale of grace,
To waft me from below,
To heaven, my destin'd place;
Then in full sail, my port I'll find,
And leave the world and sin behind.'[14]

I asked, "What makes you feel so happy today, Nathan?"
"Thinking of my Savior."
"Then you still are happy, although you are in pain?"
"Yes, sir."
"What have you thought about most, today?"
"About dying."

It was about this time, that I was sitting by his bedside one pleasant afternoon. The sun was just going down. The window of his chamber opened towards the clear red sky of the west. I saw that he was looking out of the window, and gazing intently upon a solitary cloud which was slowly passing by. I asked him if he loved to look at the sky.

"Yes, sir," he replied, but made no farther remark.

It was, either on this occasion, or some evening very much like it, that he asked if I would not like to hear him repeat the Evening Hymn. And he pronounced the verses, with the greatest propriety, now looking out, upon the clear western sky, and now closing his eyes, if the verse or line expressed a sentiment peculiarly suited to him.

THE EVENING HYMN

'The day is past and gone,
  The evening shades appear;
Oh, may I ever keep in mind,
  The night of death draws near.

I lay my garments by,
  Upon my bed to rest;
So death will soon disrobe us all,
  Of what we here possessed.

---

[14] Hymn written by Augustus Toplady.

> Lord keep me safe this night,
>   Secure from all my fears;
> *May angels guard me while I sleep,*
>   Till morning light appears.
>
> And when I early rise,
>   And view th' unwearied sun;
> May I set out to win the prize,
>   And after glory run.
>
> And when my days are past,
>   And I from time remove,
> *Lord, may I in thy bosom rest,*
>   *The bosom of thy love.'*

He then asked, "How long are you going to stay in town?"

"Until next week, I expect," said I. "And I suppose I cannot hope to see you many times more;———your friends cannot expect that you will, or hope that you may, continue long."

"Well," said he, with a trembling voice, "I hope we shall meet in a better world, and then we'll tune a sweeter"———his voice ceased,—he could say no more.

I asked him, presently, if there was anything he would like to have me tell little boys and girls after he was gone, and especially Sabbath School children.

"Yes sir," said he—and after hesitating a moment added, "Tell them to love the Savior,—and pray to Him, and read the Bible, and *not* PUT IT OFF."

I inquired if there was any particular hymn, which he liked very much, saying,—"I shall love to think of you after you are gone,—and to remember your favorite hymn often." He thought a moment, and repeated the first lines of the hymn:

> *'One there is above all others,*
> *Well deserves the name of Friend;*
> His is love, beyond a brother's,
> Costly, free, and knows no end.

24

> Which of all our friends to save us
> Could or would have shed his blood;
> But this Savior died to have us
> Reconciled in him to God.
>
> When he lived on earth abased,
> Friend of sinners, was his name;
> Now, above all glory raised,
> He rejoices in the same.
>
> Oh, for grace our hearts to soften!
> Teach us Lord, at length to love;
> We, alas! forget too often,
> What a Friend we have above.'

He afterwards, in conversation with his mother, when they were alone, desired that this hymn might be sung at his funeral.

Oct. 22. Found Nathan very feeble, though relieved, in a great measure, of his cough. I asked him how he was. He replied with a smile, "I am more comfortable today."

He gave me the Sabbath School Prayer Book for Children, which a lady had carried in to him. He opened it, and turning over the pages to the following hymn, looked up to me, expressing, by his countenance, a wish to have it read. While hearing it, he closed his eyes, and at the end of almost every verse, whispered in a low voice, "Yes, sir," as though he understood and felt the sentiment.

> 'When languor and disease invade
> This trembling house of clay
> 'T is sweet to look beyond my pains,
> And long to fly away.
>
> Sweet, to look inward, and attend
> The whispers of his love;
> Sweet to look upward to the place
> Where Jesus pleads above.

Sweet, to reflect, how grace divine,
My sins on Jesus laid;
Sweet to remember that his blood
My debt of suffering paid.

Sweet, on his faithfulness to rest,
Whose love can never end;
Sweet on his covenant of grace
For all things to depend.

Sweet, in the confidence of faith,
To trust his firm decrees
Sweet to lie passive in his hand,
And know no will but his.

If such the sweetness of the streams,
What must the fountain be
Where saints and angels draw their bliss,
Immediately from Thee!'[15]

He seemed to enjoy peculiarly the fifth verse. I read to him also, the hymn on the 108th page of the Prayer Book.

'In vain my fancy strives to paint,
The moment after death
The glories that surround the saint,
When yielding up his breath.

One gentle sigh his fetters break,
We scarce can say, "He's gone!"
Before the willing spirit takes
Its mansion near the throne.

Faith strives, but all its efforts fail,
To trace the Spirit's flight;
No eye can pierce within the veil,
Which hides the world of light.

---

[15] This hymn was written by Augustus Toplady.

26

Thus much (and this is all) we know,
Saints are completely blest;
Have done with sin and care and woe,
And with the Savior rest.

On harps of gold they praise his name,
His face they always view;
Then let us followers be of them,
That we may praise him too."[16]

I often explained verses of scripture and hymns to him, when reading and they often gave rise to very interesting inquiries and remarks from him. As I made some remarks on the third verse, he was exceedingly interested in the thought, that although we cannot look up to Heaven, and see God, and angels, and happy spirits there, yet God, and perhaps angels and spirits, can at all times look down and see us.

---

[16] Hymn by John Newton.

CHAPTER THREE

Account of his admission to the Church, which he calls 'the Meeting.'
Hymns. He is wearied with company. His sickness and suffering increase.
He is very patient. Various anecdotes. His desire to give the Author a
keepsake. Conversation. He gives the Author several little books and tracts.

Oct. 22. Thursday. For several days past Nathan has been
inviting many of his friends, as they called, to come in, this
afternoon, when Dr. Jenks was expected to come and baptize
him. Today I told him that we were afraid he would not be able
to bear a great deal of company; and that all his friends were
desirous that he should not be fatigued and confused by the
number of visitors. And that any, however much they would
wish to be present would be very sorry to come, if it should
prove an injury to him; that we were all very desirous that he
should have strength to enjoy the ordinance.

He looked up with an expression of countenance that
cannot be described, and said, "But God will give me strength
and joy."

He seemed to wish as many of his friends as possible to
come and enjoy, with him, the scene which he anticipated with
so much pleasure.

He requested me to invite several ladies, who had been
very kind to him during his sickness; and he mentioned
particularly his Sabbath school teacher and the superintendent;
but seemed especially desirous to have me call and invite Mr. P,

the gentleman, who he said, a few days before, was the first man who asked his mamma to send him to the Sabbath School. And of this gentleman he spoke very many times, with much affection.

Before leaving him this morning, I said, "Well, Nathan, I would keep as still and quiet as I could, and not talk much, so that you may have fresh strength to enjoy the service this afternoon." He looked up earnestly and said,

"I have prayed to God for strength." The same remark he had also made to his pastor when the subject had been mentioned with some anxiety on his account.[17]

Thursday Evening. Went in about six o'clock and found from twenty to thirty persons in Nathan's chamber, who had assembled to witness his baptism. Several members of Dr. Jenks's church, the ladies and gentlemen whom he had invited, and a few children, made up the little circle that were seated around him.

Little Nathan was bolstered up in the bed, so as to have a full view all over the room. Although his head ached severely, and was tied around with a white handkerchief, he seemed as pleasant and happy as he could be. His eye rested upon the visitors, one after another, as they entered the room, with an expression of countenance that no words can describe.

Just as all were seated and the room had become perfectly still, Dr. Jenks came in. A few moments then passed, in a kind

---

[17] The Examining Committee of the Church visited him, to see if he gave sufficient evidence of piety, to be received as a church member. One of the number asked him some hard questions, designed to bring clearly to view his real feelings. Mr. _____ asked, 'Well, Nathan, is it because you read in the Bible, and pray to God, and love the Savior, that you hope to go to heaven?' 'No sir,' he replied, 'it's because Christ died.'

Mr. _____ asked him, also 'Well, Nathan, on the whole, don't you think you should like to get well again?' Nathan turned his face away with an expression of disappointment that such a question should be asked, and answered, 'I don't think anything about it, sir.'

of pleasing solemn silence, which those only can truly realize, who have witnessed some such scene as this.

After some appropriate remarks addressed to little Nathan, and to the listening audience before him, Dr. Jenks read the following verses of the hymn, which Nathan had the day before requested, to be sung on the occasion.

'See Israel's gentle Shepherd stands,
With all engaging charms;
Hark, how he calls the tender lambs,
And folds them in his arms.

'Permit them to approach,' he cries,
'Nor scorn their humble name;
For 'twas to bless such souls as these,
The Lord of angels came.'

Ye little flock, with pleasure hear,
Ye children seek his face;
And fly with transports to receive
The blessings of his grace.'[18]

While a few of the ladies and gentlemen were singing these appropriate words, as it seemed, in the soft, sweet melody of the heart, Nathan turned his eyes upon his parents and little sisters, who were at his bedside. And such a look,—such an expression of countenance, it seems impossible for one who did not witness it to conceive.

The reverend pastor then offered prayer. A few verses of Scripture suited to the occasion were then read, and the Confession of Faith adopted by the church, was briefly explained. And as he listened to the explanation of the different articles as they were read, he responded in a gentle voice,

"Yes sir."

---

[18] Hymn by Philip Doddridge.

In the same manner the articles of the church Covenant were read and explained, and he replied to them, in the same low response.

The members of the church now arose, and as they were standing around his bed, Dr. Jenks administered the ordinance, and declared Nathan admitted a member of the Church of Christ.

After another prayer and hymn, this most interesting exercise was closed, and the company one after another went away. He bore the 'Meeting,' as he called it, remarkably well, and it really seemed that he received that strength from Heaven, for which he had prayed.

Friday Morning. Oct. 23. He was rocking in his mother's arms; very pale, and his forehead knit with pain. He could not smile, as he almost always did when I went in.

Soon after I entered, he had a few moments of very great pain. He laid his head back over his mother's arm, and desired her to ask me to talk with him.

I took up the Village Hymn Book, intending to read a few verses and explain them. After he had heard the two verses,

> 'Sweet glories rush upon my sight,
> And charm my wondering eyes,
> The regions of immortal light,
> The beauties of the skies.
>
> All hail, ye fair celestial shores,
> Ye lands of endless day;
> Swift on my view, your prospect pours,
> And drives my griefs away.'

I paused a moment, when he raised himself up in her lap, immediately saying,

"Is that all," and reached out his hand to take the book. After looking over the hymn, for some moments, he returned it to me, and said, "That's beautiful."

I read the remaining verses:—

> 'There's a delightful clearness now,
>   My clouds of doubt are gone;
> Fled is my former darkness too,—
>   My fears are all withdrawn.
>
> Short is the passage—short the space
>   Between my home and me;
> There! there behold the radiant place,
>   How near the mansions be!
>
> Immortal wonders! boundless things,
>   Let those dear worlds appear!
> Prepare me, Lord, to stretch my wings,
>   And in those glories share.'[19]

While he heard these verses he would occasionally close his eyes and whisper, "Yes sir," at the close of a verse.

He then laid himself down again upon his mother's arm, and said, "It's a beautiful hymn."

I then said, "Are you not too tired to hear the next hymn?" He hesitated a moment, and asked, "Is it the one right above it?"

"No," I replied, "the next after it."

"Is it the one," said he again, "O pale destroyer?"

This was the last verse of the hymn preceding the one I had read, and on the same page of the book, so that it appeared he had been reading this verse also.

It was thus:

> 'No more, O pale destroyer, boast,
>   Thy universal sway;
> To heaven-born souls, thy sting is lost—
>   Thy night, the gate of day.'

---

[19] This hymn is by Augustus Toplady.

Oct. 24. Saturday. He was easier today, but was so weak, that I did not converse much with him. He appeared, however, as tranquil and happy as ever.

I asked him, if he should like to have a hymn read.

"Yes sir," said he, and selected the following of Watts:

'Earth has engrossed my love too long!
   'Tis time I lift mine eyes,
Upward, dear Father, to thy throne,
   And to my native skies.

There the blest Man, my Savior sits;
   The God! how bright he shines!
And scatters infinite delights
   On all the happy minds.

Seraphs, with elevated strains,
   Circle the throne around;
And move and charm the starry plains
   With an immortal sound.

Jesus, the Lord, their harps employs,
   Jesus, my love, they sing!
Jesus, the life of all my joys,
   Sounds sweet, from every string.

Now let me mount and join their song,
   And be an angel too;
My heart, my hand, my ear, my tongue,
   There's joyful work for you.

I would begin the music here,
   And so my soul should rise;
Oh! for some heavenly notes to bear
   My passions to the skies.'

When he had found the hymn, before he passed the book into my hands, he looked over the first verse with such attention as to convince all around that he understood its meaning.

A lady who was present, afterwards remarked to a friend, "He seemed to be choosing what expressed his own feelings."

While the hymn was read, he listened with great attention; but company coming in, interrupted the exercise, and I soon went away.

Saturday Evening, half past 8. I have just returned from Nathan's chamber. His mother said that as soon as I left the room this forenoon, he burst into tears, and cried aloud. On asking the reason, she learned that he was so grieved that I should go away without uniting with him in prayer. He had asked me to pray, but in so low a voice that I did not hear him.

As I entered the room, this evening, he greeted me with his accustomed smile, and in answer to my question, replied,

"I am pretty comfortable, but don't feel much like talking,"——"There has been a *sight* of company here."

He was evidently quite exhausted, by seeing so many visitors.

Presently, he called his mother to his bedside and said, "Mamma, won't Mr. Abbott come and talk with me?"

I thought it not judicious to have him hear or say much, he was so much fatigued, but he requested to have a hymn read.

I read the 68th hymn, second book, of Watts.[20]

> 'Father I long, I faint to see,
> The place of thine abode.'

He listened very attentively, until I had finished, and then said,

"You may turn down a page there."[21]

I sat a few moments at his bedside, without speaking, and was deeply interested in noticing the mild and heavenly expression of his countenance. He soon turned his eyes to me, with a most lovely look and said,

---

[20] *The Psalms and Hymns of Isaac Watts* is now available from Soli Deo Gloria.

[21] To 'turn down a page' meant to fold it over at the top to make it easier to find the next time he looked for it.

"I've had this thought lately,—that if God sees fit to take me with him to heaven, I long to go."

His mother told him, that a friend would come and watch with him, if he wished it.

He seemed very much pleased and said,

"You may come tomorrow night,—if God spares me."

His pain now became very severe, and he looked up to his mother and said with a look of suffering patience,

"Oh mamma!"

"What, dear?" said she.

"I *am* tired," he replied, "will you rock me?"

A little before I went in this evening, he said to his mother, as she was laying him down on the bed,

"Oh mamma, if it was God's will, I shouldn't want to see another day."

Sabbath Evening, Oct. 25. Just returned from Mr. Dickerman's. Our little sufferer has endured a great deal of pain today. Visitors have been continually calling. Hardly an hour has passed when several strange faces were not before him, and sometimes a room full. He really seemed distressed from seeing so much company. His whole frame quivered as it were with that kind of nervous excitement, which a sick person feels after such a day.

His own account of it was truly affecting. He said, "If they would only come, one at a time, and talk a little with me,—and pray with me,—and then let me have an hour or two to rest, I could see them."

His parents felt a delicacy about forbidding visitors to see him, but requested me to spend the evening there, and excuse Nathan to any who might call upon him. It is much to be regretted that friends, in such cases, do not show their kindness and attention, in a better way than by visiting the sick chamber in great numbers and occasioning fatigue and distraction to the enfeebled sufferer, who feels unwilling to deny himself, or to have his friends deny to others, the pleasures of meeting. The sick chamber is the last place for the congratulations of many friends; it is the appropriate place for the kind and constant attention of a *few*.

Just before I came away, I stepped to his bed-side, and asked if he was not too tired to hear a few words. He replied promptly, "No sir."

I endeavored to comfort him, by directing his thoughts to the Savior, and to that rest which he hoped soon to enter, and closed my remarks, by repeating the promise,

"Him that cometh to me, I will in nowise cast out."[22]

He responded, in an audible whisper,

"Yes sir, yes sir, yes sir."

Monday Morning. Oct. 26. Found him somewhat rested from the extreme fatigue of yesterday, but still in severe pain. In a moment of respite from suffering, he asked, with a smile,

"Mr. Abbott, will you read some good hymns?

—Mamma, will you hand the hymn book?"

I read a hymn, but he was in too much pain to enjoy it, and I thought he did not follow the sentiment.

I was sitting by his side, fanning him, when he looked up to me, and smiling, asked,

"Are you busy this afternoon?"

"No, not particularly," I replied.

"Have you that map, which you brought here a little while ago?"[23]

"Yes, it is at our house."

"Can you spend the afternoon with me, and bring the map?"

---

[22] John 6:37.

[23] The writer of this journal, one day before he began to write an account of his visits, had carried in a large Atlas, containing maps of scripture places. One of the maps represented Jerusalem, and the adjacent country, such as the Mount of Olives, the Garden of Gethsemane, Mount Calvary, &c And as he read passages of Scripture, referring to those places, he pointed them out to Nathan.

He was here interrupted by a severe paroxysm of pain at his heart, and raising his eyes towards heaven, and closing them, whispered, as I thought,

"Oh! my God.———"

I could not hear any more, but in a moment his countenance resumed the same calm and cheerful expression, as before the pain came on.

The nature of his disease was such, as to occasion the severest pain. The original inflammation settled upon the heart, and caused an enlargement of that organ. The pulsations were often so rapid, that it was not easy to count them. And his whole frame would be so agitated by the violence of the action, that the bedclothes which covered him were often put in motion.

His physician, however, remarked that notwithstanding all his sufferings he never uttered a murmuring word. The nearest approach to impatience, he manifested, was once, when in great distress, as his mother was trying to do something to relieve him, he cried,

"Quick, quick, mamma, quick."

His mother was mentioning today, the case of a young man, in a neighboring town, who was very sick and expected very soon to die. He was so much opposed to anything like religion, that he was unwilling to have religious conversation in his room.

At this moment Nathan turned to me, and said, with a sad countenance, "They never had a prayer in the house."

A minister, who had visited the sick man, was a day or two before this, giving an account of his visits to Nathan, and said that he had never been requested to pray there. Nathan looked up to him, in deep concern, and said,

"Why won't you ask them, next time, if you MAY pray."

Monday Evening, 9 o'clock. Have just spent an hour with Nathan. He was more weak and exhausted than usual. I sat a half-hour by his bedside, and hardly a word was spoken. A sigh or exclamation now and then escaped him,

As "Oh, momma! Oh me."

In order to obtain a little relief by changing his position, he stood up on the side of the bed, placed both his arms around his mother's neck as she stood beside him, and laid his head upon her shoulder. This seemed in a measure to relieve his pain. He often appeared nearly as much concerned, lest he should weary others in this situation, as they were to relieve him. The tender feelings which he always exhibited towards his mother, in her unwearied and unceasing attention to him, were very apparent in every visit I made. When she was doing anything for him, which he supposed was wearisome, he often said in a most affectionate manner,

"Mamma, don't I tire you?" or "I'm afraid I fatigue you."

This evening, as I took his mother's place a little while, standing to support him, as he rested his arms and head upon my neck, he often made the same inquiries in the same sweet voice.

Before uniting with him in prayer, I asked what he wished me to pray for. He answered without a moment's hesitation,

"That I may be prepared for heaven."

He was one day standing on the bed-side, resting his head upon his grandmother's shoulder, as described above, when his mother returned from calling on a friend. She was mentioning, in the room where they were, that the person she had visited, did not believe in the reality of Nathan's apparent feelings; that she had little confidence in his piety or conversation; and said he must have learned all this by rote from his teachers, or had it written down in some book.

Nathan heard what his mother said and raising his head from his grandmother's shoulder, turned around and replied,

"So I *have* got it written down in a book, mamma, and that's the Bible."

Wednesday. Oct. 28. Nathan is more comfortable than usual today. He appeared remarkably cheerful and pleasant, a constant smile, almost, upon his countenance.

I asked him how he felt. He replied,—"Oh! I feel very happy."

I had hardly time to inquire how he had been since I saw him, before he said,

"Won't you read to me something—some verses in the Bible."

After reading he spoke of the hymn,

> 'When languor and disease invade
> This trembling house of clay.'

And wished to hear it again.

I asked him, if he knew what was meant by this trembling house of clay.

"The body," said he, "this body of sin."

While reading the other verses, I remarked, that we should never be entirely free from sin, until we reached heaven, and alluded to the verse of David,

"I shall be satisfied when I awake with thy likeness."[24]

"Yes sir," said he, with a good deal of animation, "and there's another verse,

'Oh! that I had the wings of a dove'—he hesitated a moment, and I added, *'then would I fly away, and be at rest.'*

"Yes sir," said he, "that's it."[25]

I made other remarks, while reading the hymn, something as follows: That we should always be unhappy, more or less, as long as we had sin in our hearts; but if we were the true disciples of Christ, we should be received to heaven, and there we should be freed from all sin, and perfectly happy. We shall

---

[24] Psalm 17:15.

[25] It will be seen that he quoted the sentiment of Psalm 55: 6, though not in the precise language of the text.

be without sin and in this respect like Christ, for the Scripture says, *"We shall be like Him, for we shall see him as he is."*[26]

"Yes sir," said he, "I often think of that."

"Of what?" I asked,—"of being like God?"

His only answer was,

"O! that I had the wings of a dove: then would I fly away, and be at rest."

This afterwards became a favorite sentiment; and he very often repeated it to his mother, when they were left alone.

When he had made the last remark, he looked up to me very intently for sometime and then whispered,

"Mr. Abbott, isn't there something I can give you for your kindness?"

"O, Nathan," I replied, "it has been a great pleasure, to me, to come and see you;" and I endeavored to lead his mind away from such thoughts by another remark. But he continued looking earnestly at me, and repeated with an affectionate smile,

"Isn't there anything?"

I tried still to divert him from the subject, by conversation; but when I had finished my remark, he seemed not to have listened much; or at any rate, his feeling of gratitude was upper-most, for he kept the idea of making a return steadily in view, and said,

"I can give you some little books."

I arose as soon as I could, in order to dismiss the subject from his mind, and bade him good afternoon, promising, at his request, to come in again, in the evening, as he said that would be the best time, for then nobody would be there.

Wednesday Evening. Called this evening, but Nathan was too sick to engage in conversation.

While I was sitting with him this forenoon, the boys playing in the streets, made such a noise as to make his head ache. He said to me,

---

[26] 1 John 3:2.

"Mr. Abbott, won't you ask those boys not to play so there."

I went out and called the boys around me, and told them how sick Nathan was, and what he wished them to do. Most of them did as they would be done by, and ceased making a noise, or went immediately away. But some of them would not do either. I suspect these were not Sabbath School scholars.

He said to his mother very early this morning, the first words almost that he spoke,

"Mamma, if Mr. Abbott, comes in today, I'll tell you what I want of him. I want him to find a good hymn to be sung at my funeral."

Thursday afternoon, half past 5, Oct. 29. Have just returned from a visit to Nathan; found him in great pain, yet smiling. I was but just seated at his side, when he asked with a sweet countenance,

"Do you want to talk with me a little?"

The following conversation ensued.

"Yes, Nathan," I replied, "if you think you are able to bear it; should you like to have me?"

"Yes sir."

"What shall I talk about?"

"About my Savior."

At this moment a severe pain seized upon his side, and disturbed the peaceful expression of his countenance.

I said to him, "Well, Nathan, although God sends upon you a great deal of pain, he can give you a peace within, that will make it less hard to bear."

"O, yes sir, yes sir."

"And, Nathan, it will be a joyful time for you, when you are relieved from all your pain."

"O yes sir."

"The Savior promises to be with his children,——with those that love him, when they most need his presence.—When people who do not love Him are sick, they have no consolation."

"No sir."

"But I trust He is near to you."

"Yes sir, I think he is."

"You will not have to bear your pain much longer, I hope. You will soon be where it will all be over. Do you remember the passage, *'Eye hath not seen, nor ear heard, neither have entered into the heart of man, the things which God hath prepared for them that love him?'*" [27]

I took up the Bible and read the passage, and, at his request, a few other similar texts respecting the rest of God's people. As I ceased reading, he said,

"You may turn down a page there."

While I read, he closed his eyes, and seemed to hear understandingly, as though he felt and enjoyed the true spiritual meaning.

The first four verses of Revelation 21 seemed especially to give him comfort. As he heard the fourth verse,—*"And God shall wipe away all tears from their eyes, and there shall be no more death, neither sorrow, nor crying, neither shall there be any more pain,"*—he opened his eyes, and looked upward with a smile. And frequently as I read, he responded to the sentiment, in a gentle voice,

"Yes sir."

A day or two later he asked me if I should not like to take some of his little books, to show to Sabbath School children, whenever I met them. He said he had quite a bundle of them, and would select two for me.

Today he asked his mother to give me the two which he had chosen. The names of them were, 'Little Children invited to Christ,' and 'Advice to Sabbath School Children.' A great many

---

[27] 1 Corinthians 2:9.

Sabbath School scholars, in different places, have seen these two books.

After Nathan had given me these, he said,

"Don't you want to take some of my tracts to give away? I have a great many.—O, have you *the Young Cottager*—that 's a beautiful one, —and *the Dairyman's Daughter?*" [28]

He was, at this time, sitting in his mother's arms, and, changing his position in her lap, he looked up to her and said,

"Can you hold me so, easy, mamma?"

---

[28] Both these wonderful books were written by Legh Richmond, a minister of the gospel, and they are available today in a couple different forms.

CHAPTER FOUR

Conversation with Dr. Jenks about "the Meeting." Various anecdotes and conversations. Prayer. His thoughts about Mr. P. who first led him to Sabbath School. Mr. Abbott. the author, reads and explains a chapter in the Bible. The Communion Service in his bed chamber. The author takes leave of him for a time

Friday, Oct. 30.—Dr. Jenks came in today. Nathan had been expecting him, almost impatiently. He had said several times during my visit, "I expect Dr. Jenks this morning."

When he entered, Nathan rose from his mother's lap, stood up at one corner of the fire place, in his loose flannel dress, and looked across with the greatest earnestness to his minister, who was seated in the other corner. The expression of intense interest in his countenance can hardly be conceived. He was so entirely engrossed in what he was about to ask, that he could not sit in his mother's lap. And the conversation which ensued was in substance as follows:

Dr. Jenks. "Well, my dear, did you find yourself very much fatigued by the service, the other night?"

Nathan. "The meeting? —No sir."

Dr. J. "You bore it pretty well, did you?"

N. "Yes sir,—Dr. Jenks, is the meeting finished?"

Dr. J. "What, my dear?"

N. "Is the meeting finished?"

Dr. J. "Perhaps not,—I should be very happy to have you partake of the emblems of our Lord's body and blood."

N. "I should like to very much.—I have no objections,—and my parents have no objections, you can ask my mother."

Dr. J. "I know, my dear, that they have no objections,—I suppose it would give them pleasure, and I should be very happy to administer to you the sacrament.

"What do you understand, my dear, by the Sacrament,—the Lord's Supper?—what do you suppose the bread and the wine means?"

Nathan, after hesitating a moment, replied in a lower tone of voice, *"The bread of life, and the blood of Christ."*

Dr. J. "Yes, dear, they represent the body and blood of our crucified Redeemer, and we partake of them, in memory of what he has done and suffered for us."

N. "Dr. Jenks, do you think you *shall* finish the meeting?"

Dr. J. "Yes dear, if you wish it. I shall be very happy to come after meeting, next Sabbath, and with a few Christian friends, partake with you, of the Lord's Supper. Our church will celebrate the communion, in the afternoon."

During this conversation, Nathan seated himself on a little cricket[29] beside me, and laid his head in my lap. Dr. Jenks, before leaving him, offered prayer. But Nathan in this position, when he had ended, was asleep.

Saturday Morning, Oct. 31—He was sitting in his grandmother's lap, and looked cheerful and happy. He had enjoyed a comfortable night. She said to me, as I sat down, "Nathan has been talking about getting well,—he says, if he *should* get well, it might be the means of making others believe."

He turned over in her arms towards me and smiling said,

"It isn't my wish—I was only thinking,—a kind of a dream—that if it should please my Savior to make me well—that I hoped it would make others believe what he can do."

"Why, what would you do," said I, "if it should please God to raise you up again?"

---

[29] In colonial times a "cricket" was a low foot stool.

"I would go about and tell the people about the Savior."

"What would you tell them?"

"How much he has done for them."

"But suppose they would not hear you, or would not care anything about it."

"I—couldn't—say—any—more."

"Well, Nathan, how do you think *you* should *live,* if you should get well again; what would you do?"

"I should like to be a minister of the gospel —if I could."

Visiting him again today, I found him in better strength and spirits than usual. Mr. B was holding him in his arms and rocking him, and Nathan seemed very happy. Mr. B spoke of a hymn, which he liked very much in the early part of his sickness. On reading the first verse to him, he manifested at once his great fondness for it, and desired to hear it all.

It was found in a few tattered leaves of an old hymn book. One day he was alone, and asked his mother to let him look over some old books and pamphlets that lay in the secretary. He found about a dozen leaves of hymns, and out of them selected the following, which afterwards became a great favorite. He often repeated it to Mr. B soon after the change in his feelings. The fifth verse, especially, he took great delight in repeating to himself.

> 'Jerusalem, my happy home,
> O, how I long for thee!
> When will my sorrows have an end,
> My joys when shall I see?
>
> Thy walls are all of precious stone,
> Most glorious to behold;
> Thy gates are richly set with pearl,
> Thy streets are paved with gold,
>
> Thy garden and thy pleasant green,
> My study long have been,
> Such sparkling light, by human sight,
> Has never yet been seen.

If heaven be thus glorious Lord,
Why should I stay from thence,
What folly 'tis that I should dread
To die, and go from hence.

Reach down, reach down thine arm of grace,
And cause me to ascend,
Where congregations ne'er break up,
And Sabbaths never end.

Jesus, my Lord, to heaven has gone,
Him will I go and see,
And all my brethren here below,
Will soon come after me.

My friends, I bid you all adieu,
I leave you in God's care;
And if I never more see you,
Go on, I'll meet you there.

There we shall meet, and no more part,
And heaven shall ring with praise,
While Jesus' love in every heart,
Shall tune the song,—'free grace.'

Millions of years, around may run,
Our song shall still go on;
To praise the Father and the Son,
And Spirit,—Three in One.

When we've been there ten thousand years,
Bright shining as the sun,
We've no less days to sing God's praise,
Than when we first begun.'[30]

Mr. B soon went away and left Nathan in his mother's lap. Not long after, he looked up to me with a smile and said,

---

[30] Translated from a Latin hymn of the 8th century. Author unknown. The last stanza will be familiar to many as it has been added to John Newton's most famous hymn, *Amazing Grace.*

"Will you please to hold me?"

While I held him, the following conversation, as near as can be remembered, took place.

"Mr. Abbott, grandmamma grieved me very much the other night,—she saw me crying, and thought it was because I was near my end, it grieved me very much that she should think I was crying, because I was going to die,—it wasn't so."

"Well, Nathan, she understands now, she thinks now, that you are willing to go, whenever God chooses."

"It grieved me to have her *think* so."

"But you are willing",—("Oh! yes, sir," interrupted Nathan,) "and I have no doubt, that your grandmother is very happy, now, to think, that you are so willing."

A short pause. "Mr. Abbott—, if I should die, won't you visit my mother, and talk with her?"

"I shall, certainly, Nathan."

"I want her to be a good woman,———I hope she loves the Savior some."

A pause again.

"Mr. Abbott—, when we pray, is it enough for us to say only the Lord's Prayer?"[31]

"Suppose that saying the Lord's Prayer only, was enough to please God, shouldn't we wish ourselves, to say more?"

Nathan. "Yes sir, that's the way I do. I say the Lord's Prayer, and then a little more.—O Lord Jesus Christ, give me a new heart."

I then made this remark to him, to which he made the following reply.

"How grateful we ought to be, Nathan, that God is willing to hear our prayers, and that we have been to the Sabbath School, and have learned about the Savior."

---

[31] He had made this inquiry of his mother, two or three times before. He seemed to be in doubt whether he should add petitions in his own language or not.

He was now resting in my arms,—his eyes closed, and I supposed from his appearance engaged in deep thought or devotion. At length, however, opening his eyes, and looking upward he said,

"I THINK THE LORD WILL BLESS MR. P, VERY MUCH; HE WAS THE FIRST ONE THAT ASKED MAMMA, IF I MIGHT GO TO THE SABBATH SCHOOL."

Could the teachers and friends of Sabbath Schools, have witnessed the strong emotion of gratitude, with which this infant disciple raised his eyes to heaven, and pronounced this *blessing* upon his benefactor, they would not be less active in seeking out and gathering together other stray lambs of the flock, to be nurtured in that fold—the Sabbath School, where the good Shepherd is wont to appear and take them in his arms and carry them in his bosom.

"Take heed," says the good Shepherd, *"that ye despise not one of these little ones; for I say unto you that in heaven, their angels do always behold the face of my father, which is in heaven."*[32]

And again, *"Verily I say unto you, whosoever shall give to drink, unto one of these little ones, a cup of cold water only, in the name of a disciple,—HE SHALL NOT LOSE HIS REWARD."*[33]

Nathan made some remark about his Sabbath School, which led me to ask, how many attended it.

"I don't know," said he, "when I was there I never dared to look around."

"Why?" said I.

"I thought it was wrong," he replied.

"Well, that was right; when we are receiving instruction from God's holy Word, we ought to be very attentive."

---

[32] Matthew 18:10.
[33] Matthew 10:42.

"Yes, sir; and when we do anything wrong, how it makes the *heart* feel. My *heart* seems to burn; when I first felt that I was a sinner, it seemed as if my heart was on fire; and when I talked to people sometimes, they laughed at me, and said they did not want to hear any such talk as that. They want to know why we are not all alike, (meaning, as to our being Christians or not, here, and happy or miserable hereafter,) and if they have any sorrows, they say that is all the punishment they shall have, and there isn't any punishment hereafter."

After resting a few moments he said,

"Mr. Abbott, will you talk with me about the Lord's Supper; I want to know all about it."

I read a few passages to him, on the subject, and endeavored to explain them, and when I remarked upon the bread and wine, he interrupted me saying,

"Yes, sir; when I say about this to folks, that the wine means his blood, and the bread means his body, they say it isn't so, they don't understand it. I should think when they sit at the Lord's Table, those that love the Savior,—that they would feel what he has done for them. I should think they would see the Spirit of God."

"Yes, Nathan, such a privilege is the highest means of grace we can enjoy. The Lord Jesus manifests himself to his children if their hearts are prepared for it, and it is a precious season."

"Oh!" said he smiling, "I hope you will enjoy it very much."

"Mr. Abbott, I know of one little girl, nine years old, that loves the Savior. She has been here, a great many times, and we have had delightful times together. There are two Sabbath School scholars that are inquiring what they have got to do to be saved. Mr. B, told me one went to Mr. H's house to ask him about it. I wish I could hear of one every day; I always feel better, it enlivens me up so."

His mother now came in, and he turned to her and said,

"Mamma—Mr. Abbott says he will come and see you, when I am dead and gone."

He spoke again of what his grandmother said, when she saw him crying, and said again, "It grieved me very much."

"What was it that made you cry, then, Nathan?"

"My pain was so great, that I couldn't help shedding a tear."

Saturday, P. M. Oct. 31. After exchanging a few words with him this afternoon, I remarked that another Sabbath day, the Lord's Day, was very near.

He replied, "Yes sir, the Sabbath is to be kept holy. There is one of the commandments,—*'Remember the Sabbath day, to keep it holy.'* How we used to learn them."

"Where?" I asked—"at the Sabbath School?"

"Yes sir, and at the everyday school; but it is so long since I heard them, that I forget. I used to know them all, but I can't say them now."

Saturday Evening, half past 9. About an hour since, Nathan was rocking in his mother's arms. The rest of the family had retired, and they were alone. He had appeared for sometime to be in gentle, quiet rest, but was suddenly seized with such difficulty in breathing, as seemed for a moment, during the struggle, to have terminated his sufferings.

Mrs. Dickerman, supposed that his spirit had fled, and called to a lady who occupied an adjoining room. It was just after she entered the room, that I went in.

Little Nathan looked pale and agitated, breathed rapidly and with great effort. His hand was pressed upon his side, his eyes were closed, and the whole countenance indicated severe pain.

He remained in this situation, perhaps a quarter of an hour, entirely motionless, except the tremor occasioned by the violent palpitation of the heart.

He then opened his eyes, turned them up to his mother, raised his trembling hand around her neck, and whispered faintly, "Rock." He gradually became easy again, and seemed comfortable, much as before.

As I arose to go away, he discovered that I was present, and looking around as though a little confused, said,

"Where, mamma?"

She replied, "Here Nathan," as I stood by his side. But he still looked about the room, as though he was lost. She added, "You know you was wishing Mr. Abbott to make a prayer with you this evening, and I was afraid you would be disappointed if he went away without your knowing it."

He turned to me then, and said, "Can't you stay?"

I replied, "I think you are too tired, and in too much pain to have me pray with you tonight."

"O! no sir, no sir," he quickly answered.

"Do you wish to have me pray with you?"

"O! yes sir, yes sir," he said at once.

I then repeated a few promises from the Scriptures and knelt by his side to pray. One expression used in the prayer was this. "O, Thou Shepherd of Israel, take this lamb into thy arms, and fold him to thy bosom."

He responded in a gentle whisper, "O! yes sir."

When I arose, he was asleep.

Sabbath Morning, Nov. 1. He was more comfortable, although he had suffered after I left him last night, from a return of the great difficulty in breathing.

As I entered he gave his little hand to receive me, and almost immediately said,

"Mr. Abbott, the testament is on the bed, will you read a little? Papa, will you get the map out of the drawer?" (meaning the Scripture Atlas, which he had used a few days before.)

I had at that time, pointed out to him the garden of Gethsemane, and had told him something about the scene of our Savior's suffering there. I now opened to the account of it given by Matthew, and while looking over the verses I intended to read, he, without knowing the passage I had selected, said,

"I wish you would read to me about Gethsemane."

"I was just thinking of that passage," I replied, "as one, which you would like to hear,—do you remember where the garden was, just out of the city, over——

"The brook Kedron," he added.

"Yes," said I, "and at the foot of Mount——

"Yes sir—Mamma when your arm is tired, I will sit up in your lap," interrupted the affectionate little boy.

I now read, Matt. 26:36. *"Then cometh Jesus with them to a place called Gethsemane, and saith unto his disciples, 'Sit ye here while I go and pray yonder.'"*

"How many disciples were there, Nathan?"

"Twelve."

"And he took with him Peter, and the two sons of Zebedee, and began to be sorrowful and very heavy."

"So then he took," said I, "only three of his disciples to go with him to a distant part of the garden, and left the others behind. Do you know who the two sons of Zebedee were?"

"No sir."

"I can show you where they are mentioned, in another place,—here, (turning to the 4th chap. 21st verse) *'and going on from thence, he saw other two brethren, James the son of Zebedee, and John his brother.'* You remember something about John, don't you?"

"Yes sir," he replied, "and Jesus said to Peter, *'Lovest thou me?'* [34]

"And you remember John, he was the disciple—"

"Whom Jesus loved," continued he.

I read again, v. 33. *"Then saith he unto them, 'My soul is exceeding sorrowful, even unto death. Tarry ye here and watch with me.'"*

"Do you understand what this means?" I asked.

"Yes sir," he answered.

"He was borne down," I continued, "on account of our transgressions."

---

[34] John 21:15-17.

"Yes sir," said he, "he was sorry on account of the punishment of sinners."

"Do you mean that he was a sinner?"

"O, no sir; it always seems strange to me that folks won't believe that he died for our sins."

"You recollect my reading to you in Isaiah, that he was wounded for our transgressions."

"Yes sir," said he, "and when he was brought before the—Gov-ern-or,—of the Priests, (meaning Pilate, John 19:6) he said, *'I find no fault in him.'*"

Again I read at the 39th verse, *"and he went a little further, and fell on his face, and prayed, saying, 'O my Father, if this cup may not pass from me except I drink it, thy will be done.'"*

"Do you know what this means?" said I.

"No sir: will you tell me what that is, 'Let the cup?' 'Nevertheless not as I will, but as thou wilt?' I often think of that, and say to myself, *'Not as I will, but as thou wilt.'*"

Nathan appeared very deeply interested in the subject of this conversation, and during the whole interview seemed intently engaged in the explanations which I endeavored to make.

He asked other questions and made other remarks than those that are written, but they are not remembered.

While I was reading, Mr. D, his superintendent came in, and interrupted the exercises a moment, for hardly anything seemed to give him so much pleasure as a visit from his superintendent or teacher. But he presently said,

"You may go on now."

After the subject was finished, he asked, "Now will you read about Golgotha, the place where they crucified him?"

I pointed to it on the map.

"Yes sir, I see it," said he.

After having read a few verses more, I said, "I think, Nathan, you are too tired to hear reading any longer; and I had better go and leave you to rest, that you may be prepared for the Lord's Supper."

"O, no sir, I ain't tired," said he at once.

Sabbath Evening, Nov. 1.—This afternoon has been most deeply interesting in Nathan's chamber. It is very seldom that such a scene is witnessed on earth. As I entered his room, he was just recovering from a fit of coughing, which had very much exhausted his strength. He had been rocking for sometime in his mother's arms, and supposing that she was weary he asked me to take him. As I held him in my arms, he asked me if I should not like to copy the hymn,

'O Jerusalem my happy home,'

to remember him by; and at his request I copied it in the end of his Sabbath School prayer book.

As the hour drew near when Dr. Jenks and a few members of his church were expected to come, to partake with Nathan of the Lord's Supper, he asked to be laid on the bed. He was so raised up by pillows that he could easily look around the room. The fever which flushed his cheeks, and brightened his eye, gave an unusual animation to his countenance, and although it wore an expression of excitement, it was mild and gentle. He had a violent headache, but seemed cheerful and happy. His pale thin hands were lying by his side. He asked for the hymn book, which he used to support the elbow, as he occasionally rested his cheek upon his right hand. Presently the company began to assemble. The chairs were arranged in order round the room. The little sufferer folded his pallid hands across his breast, and greeted with a peaceful countenance the different individuals as they came in.

The articles of the communion service were brought, and the table was spread before him, at the foot of the bed.

All things were now ready, and the room was still. Now and then one and another came silently in, went to the bedside, and exchanged with Nathan the look of salutation, and then took their seats. At last the chairs were all filled, and we waited in silence the arrival of the minister. Every one seemed full of emotion. Nathan's countenance expressed what no words can describe. His eye,—now passing around the room, noticed his several friends, now raised upward, and again resting on the flagon and cups, and the white napkin, which covered the consecrated bread.

At last the Reverend Pastor came, and sat before the table. The parents and sisters were at the bedside, at Nathan's right hand. His superintendent, teacher, and Mr. P, who were invited at his particular request, were present.

After a little pause, Dr. Jenks rose, and addressed himself to Nathan in nearly the following words.

"We are about, my dear boy, to celebrate an institution of *your* and our Savior."

"Yes sir," was heard in a faint whisper in reply.

"We have a description of its first establishment, in the Sacred Scriptures of the New Testament."

"Yes sir," was whispered again; and occasionally, during the few remarks that followed, the same soft response was distinctly heard around the room.

The napkin was removed from the 'emblem of His broken body, which was bruised for us,' and the meaning of the ordinance briefly explained.

While we united in 'giving thanks,' the stillness of the room was now and then broken by a stifled sigh of suffering from the little communicant.

As the bread was distributed, he put forth his hand and received a portion, in the most becoming manner.

When all had received of it, the plate was returned to the table. Dr. Jenks then rose and said,

"I thank thee, O Father, Lord of Heaven and earth, because thou hast hid these things from the wise and prudent, and hast revealed than unto babes; even so, Father, for so it seemed good in thy sight."[35]—These were the words of our Savior, on a certain occasion, when on earth, and surely we may adopt them now. O, how many wise have there been, who, in

---

[35] Matthew 11:25.

the wisdom of this world, have passed by our Lord and Savior Jesus Christ."

After the same manner the cup was distributed, Dr. Jenks addressing little Nathan thus: "We receive, my little Christian brother, these emblems of the Sacramental Table, to remind us of our Savior's love. It is not hard, my dear, for those who love the Savior, to hold him in remembrance. But O, how often is he forgotten."

After supper we sang one of his favorite hymns,

> 'When languor and disease invade
> This trembling house of clay,
> 'Tis sweet to look beyond our pains,
> And long to fly away.'

While the little circle around him were singing, Nathan laid his hands and the hymn book on his bosom, turned a most affectionate, but artless look upon his father and mother and sisters, then gently reclined his head upon the pillow and looked upward. An expression remained upon his countenance, which no language can describe, and none but a spectator of the scene can well conceive. Those who were permitted to enjoy this season, will not soon forget it.

Sabbath Evening, half after 8.—Went in to take leave of Nathan, expecting to leave the city the next day. He was much exhausted by the exercises of the afternoon, though he had enjoyed them very much. On account of his fatigue and the lateness of the hour, I made no signs of staying; and he asked,

"Mr. Abbott, can't you stay?"

"A little while," I replied; "I think you are too much fatigued to have me stay long."

"O, no sir," said he, "I wish I felt able to talk with you. You must make a prayer, before you go. Shall you go in the morning?"

"Yes, I expect I shall," said I.

"Won't you come in before you go?"

"I expect to go too early."

"What time?"

"About seven."

"Can't you come in at six?"

"Perhaps I shall not go so early; it may be bad weather."

"Does it rain now?"

"No, but it is very dark and cloudy, and does not look like pleasant weather yet."

"Mr. Abbott," he then said, after a moment's pause, "I should be very happy to talk with you, if I felt able."

"I had rather you would not, Nathan; I should like to talk with *you* a little, if you were not so tired."

"I can hear you talk, if I don't answer questions. I should like to have you.—Mamma, do I sit easy?"

"Yes, dear," his mother replied.

"Well, Nathan," I added, "I wanted to say a few words to you before I go, as we may not meet again, about some things which I should like to have you do. When you are in pain and suffering, look to the Savior'"

"O, yes sir."

"I hope he will be very near to you. He can comfort you, and give you all you need."

"O, yes sir.—Mamma, I'm afraid I tire you, don't I?"

"And, Nathan, when you think you are going to die, put your trust in the Savior; for the promise is that when we are passing through the dark valley of the shadow of death, he will be with us."

"O, yes sir; the Savior is able to support,—and willing."

"And when you say anything to anybody about the Savior and about their souls, you can pray to God for them at the same time that the truth may go to their hearts."

"O, yes sir; we can pray when we are sitting up, or lying down,—or rocking."

"Is there anything in particular which you wish to have me pray for, when I am gone?"

"Mamma, if I make you tired just lay me on the bed.— Yes sir, pray that I may be prepared for heaven, that I may keep growing in grace, and that my affliction may be sanctified to my parents and sisters, and to me."

Let it be remembered, this is the language, and I think word for word, of a babe in Christ, not eight years old. One would be almost disposed to think, that such maturity in Christian experience, could not be found in a child so young, and who had enjoyed religious privileges so short a time. But his daily appearance and conversation were irresistible evidence that he was taught indeed of the Holy Spirit, and that what he said was the expression of the real and sincere feelings of his heart.

The day after this most interesting occasion, I called and asked him how he was. As might be supposed, the previous excitement had exhausted his strength, and aggravated his pains. But he immediately replied,

"O, I feel very happy."

Here ends Mr. Abbott's Journal for the present, for at this time he left town, and was absent a fort-night.

CHAPTER FIVE

Various visitors during the Author's absence. Anecdotes. Dr. Wisner's visit. Nathan's affection for his sister. Anecdotes furnished by several individuals. His conversation with the Doctor. A Sabbath School teacher and his class go to see Nathan. His conversation with them.

During Mr. Abbott's absence, his brother and sister, Mr. and Mrs. J. Abbott, often visited Nathan and sent, in their letters to him, accounts of their visits.

The following statements are contained in a Journal kept by Mrs. Abbott.

On entering Nathan's chamber this afternoon, I found him in bed, alone, and the room darkened, except the soft light which a half opened shutter let in upon his countenance. Immediately on seeing me, he raised himself quite upright, and held out both hands, giving a very expressive look of pleasure. On his mother's entering the room, he said with much animation, "O, Mrs. Abbott has come, I am so glad;"—and turning to me, said, "I thought you would come. You can't think how much I miss Mr. Abbott.—he has been so kind, and has been here so much, that I am very much attached,—but here is his hymn book,—see it."

He had passed a distressing night, owing to pain in his side, but was then unusually free from pain, and was very cheerful; and his voice was stronger than for sometime past.

His mother said he had made himself almost sick by crying so much for Mr. Abbott, during the morning, but had since slept, and was refreshed.

Our conversation was much as follows:

On Nathan's holding the hymn book, I said, "Shall I read to you?"

"O yes;" turning over the leaves slowly; "but mamma, will you give me that piece of a book on the shelf?" His mother handed him a few torn leaves, and he immediately turned to a hymn beginning,

'Jerusalem, my happy home,'

and with much emphasis laid his hand upon it, and at its close, asked, "Isn't that beautiful?"

It suggested so strikingly to me the 21st chapter of Revelation that I turned to it, and after a simple explanation, commenced reading, selecting those verses which described particularly the New Jerusalem.

He earnestly and closely followed the reading, and at the close of the fourth verse he said softly, "Will you stop? I wish you would read me that again." At the close of the 23rd verse, he said, "Yes, the Lamb of God; that is Jesus Christ."

I was, at his request, about to sing a verse or two of a hymn, when Mrs. L and Miss P came in. I shook hands with them, and he asked if either of them was my sister.

"No, they are my friends."

Mrs. L then conversed with him as follows:

"Does it hurt you to talk, Nathan?"

"Sometimes, but not to you; it does sometimes to strangers."

(He had never seen them before.)

"You have been sick a great while, but I am glad to hear you are patient in suffering, and are so happy."

"It is the Savior does it all. He supports me in my pain."

"It is a great comfort to see our friends thus supported and to have such consolations in trial."

"Yes, but sometimes I think we ought to pity those most who are not so, and who do not love the Lord; particularly when they are sick and in pain. Are you in the Sabbath School?"

"No, I have been, and my children all go. Do you love the Sabbath School?"

"O, yes, and Sabbath School children. Where do you go to meeting?"

"To Mr. B's. Where did you go before you were sick?"

" To Dr. Jenks's, and I went a little while to Mr. B's Bible Class last winter, before I was sick the last time."

"Dr. Jenks has been a kind friend to you. Did you feel it a privilege to receive the Sacrament? I hear you have had it administered to you."

"O yes, indeed; Dr. Jenks was here last Sunday night, and I enjoyed it very much." (After a pause.) "I have lost a very kind friend,—did you know him? He has been very kind and been here very often and held me, and talked with me, and I wish he had not gone away."

I left him, finding he began to look tired, but not till he had whispered to me to "come and sing a hymn tomorrow."

For some days I visited him regularly in the morning, and twice at evening, but as he was generally suffering too much or was too feeble to talk, passed the time in reading to him, in which he always seemed to feel a deep interest and was never weary.

Sabbath Evening, Nov. 8. Visited Nathan with Mr. Abbott. He was up and resting himself in his mother's lap, and in an unusual position, and one which it seemed could not be comfortable. I sat down by him, and he very soon asked me to rub him with my hand, for he was numb. His flesh seemed to have almost the coldness of death upon it, and he spoke and breathed with difficulty. Mr. Abbott carried him in his arms till he fell asleep, and soon afterwards we left him, and I promised to call early in the morning, feeling little confidence of finding him alive. (All the conversation of this evening, Mr. Abbott has noted down.)

On Monday morning I found him sitting up in a rocking chair, apparently suffering extremely. I immediately took him up in my arms, and by rubbing and gently rocking him, some relief was afforded. He said he could not talk, but could hear me talk or read, and seemed much to enjoy some hymns I sung to him, particularly,

'Am I a soldier of the Cross?
A follower of the lamb?
And shall I fear to own his cause,
Or blush to speak his name?'[36]

At the first verse he opened his eyes, and smiled with an expression of joy as well as submission. His little sister of four years old lay in the cradle near us, sick with the measles, and very fretful and peevish. He often turned his head to look at her, sometimes saying, "O don't, dear Rebecca." "Do be patient." "I wish you loved God;" and once, though he spoke with great difficulty, "O Rebecca, if you knew who made you suffer, you would not be so impatient." He several times groaned aloud when she cried and screamed out, saying her head ached; and said once, looking at her very earnestly and affectionately, "I hope this sickness will do her good,"—Dr. Wisner came in, and Nathan immediately said, "I cannot talk, but he can talk to me, and pray with me."

Dr. Wisner writes concerning this visit as follows:—I had called a few days before, but found Nathan in great distress, and had no conversation with him; and after sitting a few minutes and conversing with his mother, had risen to go, when Nathan, who had learned that I was a minister, asked me to come again soon, when he hoped he would be better. Upon my coming in today, Nathan said, "I can't talk, but he can talk with me, and pray with me." I then spoke of the Savior's knowing all his sufferings, and sympathizing with him, repeating the text, Hebrews 4:15, *'We have not an High Priest that cannot be touched with a feeling of our infirmities.'* Nathan said, "Will you explain to me the chapter where that is?" I then read from the ninth verse to the end, of the chapter, explaining each verse

---

[36] This hymn is by Isaac Watts.

in a clear and simple manner, and dwelling particularly on the last two verses. I then asked Nathan a few questions about heaven, and why he desired to go to heaven. As soon as I commenced speaking, Nathan seemed to forget his sufferings, and listened with intense interest, and with a calm, peaceful countenance, several times whispering, "Yes, sir," though there were at times strong indications of pain from the rapidity of his pulse and the movements of his limbs, and his evident desire to have Mrs. Abbott continue to rub him. In his replies to the questions about heaven, he said not a word about its affording relief from suffering, but said he desired to go there, because there was no sin in heaven, and there all were good, and there was God and the Lord Jesus Christ. When I paused, Nathan said, "Now pray with me." I said, "What do you wish me to pray for?" He replied, "For my sister, that she may feel that God has made her sick, and be patient, and that her sickness may do her good, and bring her to love Jesus Christ."

Mrs. Abbott's account of her visits continues as follows.

On my next visit Nathan said, "I cannot talk, it makes me cough; but here is the Hymn Book and New Testament," which were by his side. I asked what chapter I should read. *"Let not your heart be troubled,"* he replied, (John 14), "I like that always. And at the close of the 27th verse, *'Peace I leave with you, my peace I give unto you, not as the world giveth, give I unto you. Let not your heart be troubled, neither let it be afraid,'"* he said with much emphasis, "How beautiful that is."

One day soon after, he said, "I think we ought to pity those who do not love the Savior, but I always feel as if I loved Christians the best who love him the most." I asked him if a gentleman whom I had seen there was pious. He said, with hesitation, *"Some,* I believe." On asking him one day if he had any message to send to Mr. Abbott who had gone out of the city, he said with much sweetness, "Tell him I am very happy, and pretty comfortable; tell him I am perfectly willing to go whenever the Lord calls for me." This seemed the habitual state of his mind, whenever I saw him afterwards, though he was suffering more at two or three subsequent visits than whenever I had seen him before.

Wednesday, Nov. 11—Sickness prevented my seeing Nathan for a week, but yesterday I found him more comfortable, though weaker. He said very little, and seemed rather absent and forgetful; expressed his sorrow that his little sister was not good, and disobeyed their mother, and said he hoped the prayers that were offered for her would be answered and that she would love the Savior.

The following letter is Mr. J. Abbott's account of the conversation alluded to in the preceding letter.

Sabbath Evening, Nov. 8. "How do you do, Nathan?" said I, as I entered.

"Pretty low, sir, this evening," answered he with a smile, rather fainter than usual. I observed also that his countenance indicated increasing weakness and pain. His breath was short and quick; his heart was beating violently, and he seemed, particularly at times during the few minutes I sat with him, to be in great pain.

"My sister is sick," said he; "won't you go and talk with her?"

I saw that his mother was holding a child in her arms by the fire. I walked towards her; the child was asleep. I made some inquiries about her, and returned to Nathan's bedside.

"Here are some little books for you," said I, "which Mr. T has sent you."

He took them, and began to turn over the leaves.

"Shall I bring you a light and show you the pictures in them?"

"No sir, I thank you."

"Should you like to have me read to you, either in these books, or the Bible, or anything else? or would it tire you?"

"No, sir, it will not tire me. I should like to have you read in the books."

I began, but found that he was in too much pain to render it expedient for me to proceed. I promised to come tomorrow and read to him, and then laid the books aside.

"Are you not going to talk to my sister?" he asked.

"She seems to be asleep," said I; "and I thought perhaps it would be best not to disturb her."

He made no reply.

After this he was very restless and seemed to be suffering. Once I went away from his bedside a minute and he began to cry, evidently from pain.

"Do you suffer much pain, Nathan?"

"Yes, sir, a good deal."

"Do you know why God causes you to suffer so much?"

"Sir?"

"Do you understand why God brings suffering upon his children in this world? Why he makes you undergo so much pain?"

"To do me good."

"But what good does it do you to lie here and suffer from day to day?"

"He sanctifies it."

I then began to talk to him, in a low whispering voice, about the advantages of sickness, and perceiving that he seemed to become easier, I placed my hands over his eyes, allowed my words gradually to die away, and then hushed him to sleep. I left him with his pale cheek resting upon his little hand, enjoying a peaceful and quiet slumber.

The next letter from Mr. J. Abbott contains an account of his visit the next Sabbath evening.

Sabbath Evening, Nov. 15.—I found him evidently more reduced by suffering than I had ever before seen him. His hands and feet were cold and numb, his breath very short, his pulse quick; and he suffered much from pains in his side and in his limbs.

His grandmother told me that our visit the other day, and particularly my reading to him a part of a letter I had received from his friend Mr. G. Abbott, revived and cheered him very much. When I left him that evening he was asleep; when he awoke he called aloud for me, and seemed quite disappointed to find I was gone.

As I sat over him this evening, I observed that after a little time he grew more easy, I said, "Cannot you go to sleep, Nathan?"

"If I do, you will go away," replied he with a smile.

I carried him about the room, and gradually lulled him to sleep. In attempting, however, to place him upon the bed, he awoke, and soon seemed to suffer considerable pain. He kneeled up in the bed and began to fix the pillows. I asked him if I could help him. "No sir," said he, "I want to fix them *my* way." He placed them in a peculiar manner, with a dexterity which implied that he had thus sought for relief from pain very often before, and then laid his head upon them with his cheek upon his hand, and looked up to me with one of his characteristic smiles, expressive of perfect peace and contentment, if not of happiness.

When I was about to leave him, I bade him good night, and said, "I hope you will have a comfortable night, and will not suffer much pain; though I do not care so much about that, as that God should be near to you and give you peace at heart."

"Nor I," said he, with a rising inflection which is lost in writing the words, but which spoke entire and happy resignation to God's will.

The following account was furnished by Mr. B, a gentleman who first visited Nathan after his interest in religion became deep and personal. Nathan was strongly attached to him, and very often spoke of him when absent, with great delight, showing how gratefully he remembered his Christian friends. Mr. B was with him the morning that he died.

The first time I visited Nathan, he wanted me to pray for him, and when the question was put, "What shall I pray for?" he answered, "That God would give me a new heart, and that I may love the Lord Jesus Christ."

I then put the question, "Do you think you are a sinner when so young?"

He answered, "Yes sir, I know that I am a sinner, and I know that I must love Jesus before I can be happy, for he has loved me."

I then asked, "Who told you Nathan, that the Lord Jesus has loved you?"

He replied,—"My teacher,—and I have read it in the Bible."

He then took up the New Testament and desired me to read the third chapter of John.

At another time he said to me in conversation, "I always feel happiest, when I am praying, and I love to hear people pray.—O! How I feel when I hear a minister pray."

Always when I visited him, he would say, soon after my entering the chamber, "I want you to pray with me before you go away."

When I asked him how he felt, he would often say, "Miserable in body, but O, how happy in my soul, for Jesus is most lovely to me."

"Well, my dear, don't you suffer a great deal?"

"Yes sir," he answered, "but nobody can suffer as much as Jesus did for me."

I asked him, if he felt willing to die, and leave his father, and mother, and sisters?

"Yes sir," said he, "I can leave all to be with my Savior. Death has no terror to me now. Jesus took little children in his arms and blessed them, and said *'Suffer little children to come unto me.'* I would not give up my hope in Christ for the world."

His mother says that the general tenor of his conversation during the first part of his sickness was like the above.

A lady, Miss S, who was a frequent visitor in Nathan's chamber, has prepared an account of her interview with him. It is as follows:

When I first visited him, I said, "My dear, I understand that the Lord has been very good to you."

He said, "Yes, my Savior is very precious."

"What reason do you think you can give, that you have a hope in Christ?"

He said, "Because I love the Lord Jesus Christ; and love to pray, and read his Holy Word."

"But," said I, "Did you not always love the Lord Jesus Christ?"

"No, Ma'am," he replied, "I was a wicked boy; I did not love to pray and read the Bible, and now I want to be where my Savior is."

"And are you willing to die and leave your father and mother, and little sisters?" I asked.

"Yes Ma'am."

"Why are you willing to die?"

"Because I *now* only think of Christ in my heart; but there I shall be where he is, and shall be like him, and shall see him as he is."

I then asked him, where he found encouragement.

He said, "In the Bible, where Christ says, *'Suffer little children to come unto me, and forbid them not.'*"

At another time, I called with Mrs. C, and her granddaughter from New York. Mrs. C, asked him if he was not weary of having so much company."

He answered, "O! no, Ma'am, I love Christians."

"Why do you love Christians," she asked.

"Because," he replied, "they love my Savior."

She then said, "My dear, I am going to New York—I am superintendent of a Sabbath School there, and I shall tell them I have seen a little boy, a Sabbath School scholar, who will probably die. Have you any message to send them?"

His countenance brightened up, as he said, "O! tell them to love the Lord Jesus Christ, and to pray to Him, and to love his Holy book."

"And what will they gain, by all that?"

"Why a new heart, and that will prepare them for the kingdom of Heaven."

Mrs. C then asked, "Do you think, that all who visit you are Christians?"

"Some," he replied, *"don't believe the Bible."*

"How do you know?" said she.

"They say they don't believe in a change of heart," he answered.

"Do you think, my dear, that you have a new heart?"

"I hope I have."

"What makes you think so?"

"Because I love my Savior."

Mrs. C, then said, "This little girl, (her granddaughter, who was then standing at his bedside), is going to New York, and will tell the Sabbath School scholars that she has seen you, but she will never see you again."

Little Nathan then took her by the hand, and said to her, "Read your Bible, pray to the Lord Jesus, love your Savior, and then you will go to heaven."

Miss S, describes a conversation, during another visit she made to him, thus:

I said, "Nathan how many wearisome days and nights do you think you will have to pass through?"

He looked up at me with a smile and answered,

"Just as many as the Lord sees fit; perhaps it will be his will to take me tonight, if not, I am willing to stay."

He then asked, if I had ever been sick.

I told him I had, and he then added, "Did you ever feel when you was in pain, that Christ was above everything else?"

I told him, "Yes;" and he replied, "Just so I feel this morning; I have had a very sick night, but I love my Savior better than I ever did."

I then told him I was going to see a poor sick woman. He asked, "Does she love the Savior?" I replied that I hoped she did.

"Then she's *rich*," said he.

Nathan often, very often, made remarks which showed in a striking manner his entire willingness to be at God's disposal, to live, and suffer, or to die. Many little anecdotes, illustrating this, have been preserved, which were written down in the journal as they occurred. They were of course interspersed through the whole of the original manuscript. Many of them have been introduced in the Memoir, wherever the subject suggested them. Several others, preserved by different individuals, follow here.

On one occasion, a lady, Mrs. V, who had shown him much kindness, and to whom he was very fondly attached, was present when several others were standing round his bed. His sufferings at the time were so great, that some present could scarcely restrain their tears, and one in the room made some such remark as this: "Dear little sufferer." Nathan heard it, and after they went away, said to his mother,

"They call me a little sufferer, but I think I'm happy."

At another time, when his physician came in, Nathan called him to his bedside, and asked him to sit. He then said,

"Doctor F, do you think I shall get well?"

"I don't know, Nathan," he replied; "should you like to get well again?"

Nathan answered, "If it is God's will, I am willing to get well or to die."

The conversation which then took place was, as nearly as can be remembered, in the following words:

"Doctor, won't you please to pray with me?"

"Perhaps your minister will be in this afternoon."

"Do you ever pray?"

"Yes, Nathan, I hope we all pray."

"Was you ever a Sabbath School teacher?"

"Yes, when in college."

"Well, Doctor, won't you please to read a hymn?"

"When I call again, if you will have one ready that you like, I shall be very happy to read to you. What books do you like to read best?"

"The Bible and *Saint's Rest.*"[37]

"Why do you, like the Bible so much?"

---

[37] Some friend had presented him with Richard Baxter's *Saint's Everlasting Rest*, which was a source of the greatest enjoyment to him.

"Because," said he "it is the word of God, and it says, *'Suffer little children to come unto me.'* There it is hanging up there," pointing to a picture over the fire-place, of the Savior, calling little children to him, and taking them in his arms.

The hymn which he had selected when the doctor called again, was

'I would not live alway; I ask not to stay
Where storm after storm rises dark o'er my way,'

At another time some one asked him if he was willing to die. He made the same submissive answer as before, and added,

'Sweet to lie passive in his hand,
And know no will but his.'

His mother has written the following anecdote:

In the early part of Nathan's sickness, when his friends called in to see him, they would say to me, "He suffers very much." After they had left the room he would say to me, "Mamma, I don't like to hear them say I suffer; they don't think how much Christ suffered, if they did, they wouldn't think I suffer much; no one suffers so much as Christ did." This he often repeated.

Nathan once said to his grandmother, that he should go to heaven when he died. She told a lady, one of her neighbors, of it, but the lady thought Nathan did not know enough about such things to tell even how he should get to heaven. His grandmother asked him the question. He replied, "Why grand-mamma, my body will be buried in the ground,—my spirit will ascend into heaven."

Once while suffering very severe pain, he was heard several times to groan. As his mother looked upon him in his distress, he said, "I don't know as I do right to groan so, mamma,—but the Savior groaned, didn't he?"

Speaking one day of those who did not care anything about religion,

"Why," said he "they do not think about their Savior, when *they have nothing else to do.*"

She also adds, when I have been rocking him, I have said to him, "How you are afflicted Nathan." He would say,

'Sweet affliction, that brings my Savior near.'

The sentiment he here expressed was contained in a hymn, which a lady had given him, 'On affliction.' Mrs. H, whom he very affectionately loved, gave him the copy. He became very fond of the verses, and often had them read to him, but still oftener repeated the sentiment of the last two lines in each verse. A little while before he died he gave the copy to one of his friends to remember him by. It begins thus:

'In the floods of tribulation,
While the billows o'er me roll;
Jesus whispers consolation,
And supports my fainting soul.
Sweet affliction, That brings Jesus to my soul.'

A lady writes thus: I was in the habit of visiting that dear child from time to time, and took great pleasure in so doing.

One day I asked him if he could say to me that he was willing to die and leave his father, and mother, and sisters, and all the pleasant things of this world, and trust only in Christ.

He looked up, with his accustomed smile, and said, "Yes, to be sure I can."

I then said to him, "There are many precious promises for children. Our blessed Lord, when on earth, took little children in his arms and blessed them, and said, *'Of such is the kingdom of heaven.'*"

At the same instant, he pointed to the mantel piece, where hung a representation of it and said, "Look! There is a picture of it, which I lay and look at often, and it is very delightful to me."

Once during his sickness, some one was conversing with him about his affliction. And as a number of children were heard at play in front of the house, he alluded to his confinement and suffering, while others were out of doors, enjoying themselves. And he asked Nathan if he didn't want to be out playing with the others.

He answered very mildly, "I don't care about it; I can pray for them that they may love the Lord Jesus Christ."

A lady writes; I once asked him how he could bear so much suffering and not complain. He answered,

"With Christ to support me, I can bear all things."

And when I asked him whether he had any doubts and fears, he replied, "No Ma'am, I can put all my trust in Jesus."

Mrs. H, another of his friends, made the following memorandum of one of her visits. I asked him if he did not wish to die. He answered, "I am willing to suffer, or willing to die; I have no choice,—I long to be with my Savior." I then asked why he wanted to go and be with his Savior. He answered, "No sin, no pain there." I then asked what was his greatest trial. He replied, "That I don't love and serve the Lord as I ought."

A Sabbath School teacher has given the following account of two of his visits to Nathan:

About six weeks before his death, one of my scholars, as I was speaking to the class of the importance of early piety, requested me to go with them and see Nathan; informing me at the same time, that many teachers went with their classes, and also telling me that he was a cousin to one of my class. After learning that Nathan was gratified to have Sabbath School teachers visit him, I told them we would go after meeting in the afternoon. We accordingly went. I was introduced to him as his cousin Roger's teacher. His pleasure was great on hearing this. After stating to him that the children wished to see him, he bade us welcome.

The three last visits I made, he said, each time, on my entering, (with one of his expressive smiles) "There's Roger's teacher."

To me he said, "You are a Sabbath School teacher?"

I answered, "I am."

"Are these your scholars?"

I answered, "Yes."

"See, here is a pencil Mr. Abbott gave me to write the texts of Scripture and hymns with."

After saying something to each of the children, he had a distressed turn, which lasted for a few minutes. Soon he revived. I said, "You suffer a great deal of pain."

"O, yes sir," he replied.

"Do you feel happy in all your sufferings, when you remember what our Savior suffered for us?"

He replied, "We do not suffer anything compared with what he suffered for us—nor half so much as we deserve."

On my saying that in heaven there is no sickness or pain, I asked him how he felt in view of it.

"Happy," was his reply.

I asked him if he was willing to leave all and go to Christ.

He answered quickly, "Yes sir."

On my next visit, he was much worse, and could say but little. But his countenance told his feelings.

I asked him, if, now he was walking through the dark valley of death, he feared any evil.

"No sir," he replied.

He evinced his love for the ordinances of God by his remarking "Next Sabbath is Communion at Dr. Jenks's, and I expect he will come here;" and invited me to attend—adding, "I should like to have you come."

Observing us in tears, he said,

"What are you crying for," adding, "You must not cry for me."

He gave each of us a tract. To me he gave *the Young Cottager*, saying, "That is an excellent tract;" adding also, "I like them."

CHAPTER SIX

The Author returns. Nathan's proposal about a little school. His great suffering. Symptoms of approaching death. Devotional exercises. He gives away his playthings and other little property. He invites a little girl to go to Sabbath School.

Mr. Abbott—had now returned to the city, and his journal was resumed.

Sabbath Evening, Nov. 22—Nathan was in great pain this evening, but soon after I went in, asked me to read a hymn.

I inquired if there was any one in particular he would like.

"Yes sir," he replied, "the one you spoke about yesterday."

"I don't remember which it was," said I; "was this the one?"

> 'Sweet was the time when first I felt
> The Savior's pardoning blood.'[38]

"Yes sir."

> 'Applied to cleanse my soul from guilt,
> And bring me home to God.'

I repeated the hymn slowly, and explained to him the verses. At the close of the last one

> 'Rise, Lord, now help me to prevail,
> And make my soul thy care;

---

[38] This hymn is by John Newton.

I know thy mercy cannot fail,
Let me that mercy share.'

he said, "Do you think he did, Mr. Abbott?"

He requested me also to read a chapter, saying, "I wish I could hear one read and explained every day; I should know a great deal about the Scriptures."

"God can *teach* you Nathan," said I, "by his Spirit."

"Yes sir," he said, "*he has taught you.*"

"I hope he will teach me," I replied, "for we depend always upon Him for all our good thoughts."

"Yes sir," said he; "you would not have come to see me again, if the Lord had not put it into your heart."

He then desired me to read about the Savior, when he was young. I turned to the second chapter of Matthew, and endeavored to explain it as I read.

At the 8th verse '*And he sent them to Bethlehem and said, "Go search diligently for the young child, and when ye have found him, bring me word again, that I may come and worship him also."*'

I asked him why he supposed Herod wanted to know.

"That he might go and believe on him," said he.

But at the 16th verse, '*Then Herod, when he saw that he was mocked of the wise then, sent forth and slew all the children that were in Bethlehem,*' he said, "Now I know what Herod wanted."

"What?" I asked.

"To kill Jesus," he replied.

Sabbath Morning, Nov. 29.—Last night was rather a more comfortable one for little Nathan than the preceding, yet he is still in much pain.

He said to me, this morning, "Do you ever have little children come together around you, and have a kind of little school?"

"Yes," said I, "I very often get them around me, to talk with them and tell them stories."

"Why won't you come this—afternoon," said he, "and bring some little children, and we will have a little school."

"I should like to come,—very much,—but perhaps your parents would prefer not to have us."

"O yes, they are perfectly willing," said he, "will you come and talk with them, and I will talk with them too."

"Well," said I, "we will see if we can find some children to come."

Presently he asked for the hymn book, and after turning over the leaves very hastily a few moments, as if trying to find a particular hymn, he said, giving the book to me,

'Till late I heard my Savior say,'

Afterwards, he requested me to read a passage which he had marked in Baxter's Saint's Rest,—*On Heavenly Meditation.*

His little sister was quite sick today, and his mother was trying to persuade her to take some bitter medicine, which she was very unwilling to do. Nathan was to take some of the same kind, which he did very pleasantly indeed, without objecting at all, and then whispered to me,

"Our Savior drank vinegar and gall."

This afternoon Nathan was laboring very much for breath, and his face was swollen sadly; but he did not seem to mind it much. He asked again for the hymn book, and said,

"Now won't you read me the hymn you like best."

He spoke again about the meeting for children, but there had been no opportunity to invite any during the day.

"Well," said he, "we can have it tomorrow, and then I can see some of the little girls from the school," meaning the Mt. Vernon School, of which he often spoke. Several of the scholars had often been to see him, and had made him presents of grapes, oranges and books, during his sickness. He was very much attached to them, and remembered their kindness with much gratitude.

He wished me to read a chapter, and being asked what passage he would like, replied, "About the star of Bethlehem."

I had said something to him on the subject before.

A very severe fit of pain soon came upon him, and he asked to be carried around the room, as his friends often carried him, in their arms. As his head lay upon my shoulder, I could hear him whispering to himself, in his great distress,

"O Lord,"—"have mercy,"—"Lord Jesus,"—"O dear."

A little while after, I was conversing with Nathan's father, about the sermon he had heard at Hanover Street Church, respecting the Jews, and something was said of the wonderful fulfillment of prophecy in their dispersion over the world. Nathan began a sentence, "And the Jews,—they——"

But his feeble voice died away, and we could not hear any more. Afterwards, however, when it was said, as we continued the conversation, that it was in consequence of their many sins, their crucifying the Savior, &c. he said, in an audible voice,

"That is what I was saying."

A gentleman shortly after called in, and while addressing Nathan, said that he must trust in God in his severe suffering, and his affliction would then work out for him a far more exceeding and eternal weight of glory.[39] But as he looked upon the little patient sufferer, he was much affected and wept. Nathan saw it, and said,

"Are you crying for *my* pain?" And as the gentleman answered, Nathan rejoined, "You mustn't mourn for me."

Wednesday, Dec. 14. After a fortnight's absence, I called again today upon Nathan. There has been a great change in his appearance, since I last saw him, His countenance has become very pale and deathlike, his cheek swollen, his eyes prominent, and all his features indicate approaching dissolution.

After I had waited a few moments, until some company had retired, I took my seat once more at the bed-side of this lovely Christian. He looked up with a smile, and said, as his first address to me,

---

[39] See 2 Corinthians 4:17.

"I have remembered your words."

"Have you," I asked, "which words?"

"Whom the Lord loveth, he chasteneth,"[40] he replied.

I had written him a short letter during my absence, and this was one of the texts which I had quoted, for him to bear in mind.

Friday Morning, Dec. 16. As soon as I looked in upon him today, he began with his usual smile,—"I have some good news,—there are two or three who are inquiring the way to be saved."

"Where?" I asked.

"At Dr. Jenks's Sabbath School."

After a short interval, he said,

"You can read a chapter and explain it to me pretty soon."

While looking over my little Village Hymn Book, which I left with him, when I went away to find a hymn to read, he said,

"I have taken a great deal of comfort reading there."

I asked him, which gave him the most pleasure, or made him happiest, reading the Bible, or hymns, or prayer.

"Praying," he answered.

He very soon asked for prayers. I said to him, "what do you wish me to pray for?"

"My parents."

"Is there anything else?"

"That, I may be prepared for heaven."

"Is there anything else?"

"That the Lord might ease my pain."

I repeated the question once more, and he answered,

"For Sabbath School children."

Sabbath Morning, Dec. 20. Nathan requested me to spend the forenoon with him, and I did. I said to him, "I have just been to visit your Sabbath School."

"O, have you," said he, "What, Hawkins Street?"

---

[40] Proverbs 3:12; Hebrews 12:6.

At his request, I opened the Bible and read a few verses in the twenty-first chapter of Matthew relating to the little children who cried in the temple, *'Hosanna to the Son of David.'*[41]

I explained to him the account of the people's strewing their garments in the way. He exclaimed,

"O yes sir, I have seen it,—the picture,—in a little magazine."

He then asked, "Will you read a hymn out of *this* book," looking at one on which he was leaning with his elbow. It had recently been given to him by a lady, and he valued it very highly. As I took the book, he said, "That one, mamma,

'I would not live alway,'

—you know it."

'I would not live alway: I ask not to stay,
Where storm after storm rises dark o'er the way;
The few lucid mornings that dawn on us here,
Are enough for life's woes, full enough for its cheer.

I would not live alway, thus fettered by sin;
Temptation without and corruption within;
For the rapture of pardon is mingled with fears,
And the cup of thanksgiving, with penitent tears.

I would not live alway; no, welcome the tomb,
Since Jesus has lain there, I welcome its gloom;
There sweet be my rest, till He bid me arise,
To hail Him in triumph descending the skies.

Who, who would live alway, away from his God;
Away from yon heaven, that blissful abode,
Where the rivers of pleasure flow o'er the bright plains,
And the noon-tide of glory eternally reigns :

Where the saints of all ages in harmony meet,
Their Savior and brethren, transported to greet:
While the anthems of rapture unceasingly roll,
And the smile of the Lord is the feast of the soul.'

---

[41] Matthew 21:15.

The third and fourth verses were his particular favorites. He used very often, when alone with his mother, to repeat the first lines, slowly and with a great deal of emphasis.

Dec. 25. From this time, until his death no regular journal was kept. The facts obtained have been principally taken from the verbal statements of his mother, with the exception of the copious minutes of her visits which a lady has kindly furnished.

Many friends have also related little anecdotes of facts respecting his few last days. But the kindness of so many friends has been manifested, that it is found impracticable to give due acknowledgement to all.

On the afternoon of Christmas day his four cousins came to see him. When the time of their visit had nearly expired, just before tea, and they were soon to return home, Nathan took an opportunity when his mother was very near him, to whisper to her,

"Mamma, are you willing I should give away my things, this afternoon?"

"What things, my dear?" she replied.

"My playthings."

His mother gave him permission, and he then called Roger, his little cousin, about ten years of age, to him, and said,

"Roger, I'm going to give you my sled, and I want you to keep it to remember me by, and be a good boy,—and mind what your teacher says, and obey your parents."

He gave also to Roger a book which he selected from his little library.

To George, a younger cousin, he gave his whip and a book.

To Charles, his cap and a book.

To Susan, he gave his Sabbath School hymn book, and said to the others nearly the same, that he did to the first.

Not many minutes after this, some of his little cousins were making more noise in the room than he could well bear, and Nathan said in a low tone to his mother, as she came up very near to him, "Mamma, I do love my cousins so,—but they make my head ache." He then said to one of them, "You've been a naughty boy, Charles, and I don't know as I shall let you carry my cap home *tonight*." But afterwards he whispered to his mother, "Mamma, you may give it to him,—I only told him so."

He gave the most indubitable evidence of sincerity, in his affection for others. One day a gentleman, one of his friends, was present,—who happened to have a slight cough. Nathan noticed it, and said he was sorry, and wished he had some spermaceti candy,[42] for he said that was very good. A third person heard Nathan express this wish, and very soon after when the company had retired, a little parcel was left at the door for Nathan containing the candy he desired.

The person, doubtless, who heard the wish, supposed Nathan wanted it for himself. He however insisted upon his friends taking a generous portion of his present.

Any nice thing that was sent to him, he was ever ready to divide with his sisters. Often, very often, have I heard him say,

"Mamma, won't you give Maria or Rebecca a piece of that orange, or one of those figs, or some of the grapes."

When even his mother was preparing anything particularly good for him, he would ask, "Mamma haven't you got some for Mrs. S," an old lady who lived in the same house.

His mother says, he would often say in such eases,

"Mamma, ain't you going to give Mrs. S some?"

One day, about this time, another little cousin, near his own age, came to see him, but not being much accustomed to a sick chamber, and struck with Nathan's pale face, he was unwilling to go to the bedside.

Nathan tried to persuade John to come and take him by the hand, but could not succeed.

---

[42] Spermaceti is a solid waxy substance obtained from sperm whales and other marine animals, and used mostly in ointments for healing.

At length John's Sabbath School teacher, who was present, took little John by the hand and they went together, and sat at the side of the bed.

Nathan then asked the teacher, "Is John a good boy?"

"Sometimes he is; he *can* be a very good boy."

"Does he get his lessons well?"

"Pretty well, generally."

"Do you ever talk with him about the Savior?"

"Yes, sometimes."

"Won't you talk with him more about the Savior?"

He manifested his interest in children, very strikingly and in various ways, in conversation with them, with parents and teachers.

His mother says he almost always inquired of his visitors, whether they were Sabbath School teachers, and when this was the case, invariably asked such questions as these:

"Do you ever tell them about the Savior? Do you think they know there is a Savior? Do you ever tell them they have got to die?"

Mrs. H made the following minutes of one of her visits. I write from his lips.

Nov. 22. "Tell them (children) to put their trust in the Savior, and believe in the Lord Jesus Christ and read the Bible, and not play on Sundays. You must tell them to pray for a new heart, and put their trust in the Savior, or they won't go to heaven." He then quoted the lines,

> 'Tis religion that can give
> Solid pleasure while we live;
> After death its joys will be
> Lasting as eternity.'

A lady called with a little girl, to see him. In the course of the conversation, he asked if the little girl attended the Sabbath School. She replied that she did not. He then asked the lady, who was at his bedside, to stand away, and beckoned to the little girl to come to him, and said to her,

"You *must* go to the Sabbath School, and learn to read, and read your Bible, and love your Savior."

She went immediately to the Sabbath School, and a little while afterwards, when Nathan had been a short time dead, she asked if Nathan knew, now that he was in heaven, that she went. And on receiving an answer, said,

"If he was here *now*, I could tell him that I go."

And who knows but this little one may become in truth one of the lambs of the flock, and may on her dying bed, have occasion to pronounce the same blessing upon him, that Nathan did on Mr. P, the gentleman who first found little Nathan and invited him to the Sabbath School.

CHAPTER SEVEN

His usual position in bed. A lady reads the prayer for a sick child from the Church Prayer Book. Nathan's interest in it. A painter takes his miniature. Interesting conversation with his father. He converses cheerfully about his approaching death. He gives his knife to his father, and a book to his mother, for them to remember him by. His last conversations. His death and funeral.

A lady, who visited him in December for the first time, has made copious minutes of her interviews, from which the following is extracted:

In December, 1829, one afternoon, I was invited by a lady to accompany her on a visit to the little child of whom I had heard so interesting an account.

We found the little sufferer evidently much wearied with the frequent calls of visitors, and anxious to be relieved from the presence of all but his mother. I asked him if he suffered much pain. He answered, "Yes;" and that he "wished I would come and sit with him some other time." We retired almost immediately, the child saying as we went, "Come again."

The next day about eleven o'clock, I went to pass a short time with him. He was much distressed, and unable to lie down. He sat upon the bedside. A chair was placed before him, with a pillow resting lengthwise across the top of it. He was leaning his head upon a Bible, which he kept in its place as it lay upon the pillow, by holding his arms around it. It was in this position that I generally saw him, as he was able to lie down but seldom, and then only for a very short time.

His little sister, who was playing about me, took out a small prayer book from my work bag. He seemed much pleased with some little pictures it contained; one, of Moses receiving the Ten Commandments, and another of an angel playing upon a harp, a frontispiece to the Psalms of David. As I was explaining the pictures, Nathan seemed to forget his pain, and exclaimed with animation, and with an expression of countenance I cannot forget, "O, let me see it."

He took the book, laid down on the bed, and appeared for a short time with his eyes riveted on the picture. Then turning the leaves gently over, he suddenly exclaimed,

"O, precious book! Will you lend it to me?"

He then sat up as before, put it with the Bible on the pillow which supported him, and laid his head on them both.

Turning his face then toward me, he said,

"I will find you some hymns, and you shall sing to me."

Singing had been spoken of before, by his mother and me. He selected from the Village Hymn Book the following:

> 'When languor and disease invade,
> This trembling house of clay;'

He wished it to be read. At the lines

> 'Sweet to look upward to the place,
> Where Jesus reigns above,'

his face glowed with delight, and his whole soul seemed absorbed in the thought. At the third line of the last verse but one, he began to repeat after me with much feeling

> *'Sweet to lie passive in his hand,*
> *And know no will but his.'*

He continued to repeat after me till I finished,

> 'If such the sweetness of the streams,
> What must the fountain be;
> Whence saints and angels draw their bliss
> Immediately from THEE.'

He then selected the following

> 'One there is above all others,
> Well deserves the name of Friend.'

He expressed much feeling when the last verse was read

> 'Oh, for grace our hearts to soften!
> Teach us Lord, at length to love;
> We, alas ! forget too often,
> What a Friend we have above.'

His physician then entered the room, and while he was conversing with his patient I retired to another part of it, and employed myself in copying the hymns I had just read. When I had finished, I overheard the question, "Do you feel willing?" and saw Nathan's sweet expression as he said, "Yes, quite willing."

His mother afterwards informed me that the doctor had then, for the first time, told him of his true situation, and of the near approach of death. The mention of approaching death *at any time* excited in him only pleasant emotions.

Nathan was then showing him the prayer book, and I went up to them and in answer to a few words and an inquiring look from him, I said he might keep it while he lived. He exclaimed, with childish delight, "Do you hear, mamma, what she says? She says she has got another, and I can leave this a parting present to you."

After the physician went away, I sang to him the hymn,

> 'I would not live alway, I ask not to stay
> Where storm after storm rises dark o'er the way.'

He expressed much delight both in his countenance and manner, and during the last verse no one who saw him would suppose he felt pain, notwithstanding his pale face. He then said,

"Will you write it for me, so that I can read it myself?"

Some of his friends had printed letters (with the pen) and sent to him. They were sometimes borrowed by his friends, and Nathan often asked for them, and seemed unwilling to have them absent. I carried in the afternoon a small edition of the Episcopal Hymns, and several little books presented to me by a friend for him.

Very soon I went, according to my promise, to spend a day with him. He looked very ill, more so than when I saw him before. He seemed very forgetful, and at first did not know me; and said, "Mother, I think she had better stay only a little while."—When she told him who it was, and that he had invited me, and that I would sit by him, he appeared gratified, and said, "Then, mother, you can do your work now, and she may sing me to sleep."

But he showed no disposition to rest, and suffered so much that it was difficult at times to restrain one's feelings. *Yet he was patient.* He showed much regard for the feelings of others, and much gratitude for any little services rendered. He spoke with much affection and gratitude of several friends, and particularly of those who had visited him often.

Mr. B made several short visits during the day. Once Nathan said to him, "Mr. B, I'm afraid that all who come to see me do not *feel* that they are sinners, though they say so."

Mr. B said, "We ought not to judge," and made some other remark; when Nathan replied,

"But, Mr. B, I do think that I *feel*, (putting his hand on his heart) that I am a sinner."

In the course of the day he selected the hymn for me to sing—

> 'See Israel's gentle Shepherd stands
> With all engaging charms,'

And also—

> 'When I can read my title clear
> To mansions in the skies.'

90

'I would not live alway,' seemed to be his favorite hymn.

At one time, being in great distress of body, he cried out, "I wish you would kneel down, and pray God to ease this pain." I took my little prayer book, and used the prayer for a sick child, making it applicable to him by words of my own. After being a little relieved, he said, not knowing that I had made any alteration in it,

"I suppose that if you read a prayer, that reading a prayer does good sometimes."

I told him that if the *heart* prayed, it certainly did good; but that if the *heart* did not pray, God would not hear what we said. He then said with much feeling,

"I am very glad that reading a prayer does good, because mother can read that little prayer for me when my friends are not here; and I think *her heart* will pray for me," and requested me to mark the place.

A little after this, he asked for my name. His mother said he wanted to know my Christian name. I told him Sarah. He said, "I must call you Sarah." Before, he always called me Lady.

Once, after several hours of extreme suffering, he had an interval of relief. But during his distress he spoke of his mother with great anxiety, and mentioned with gratitude, the promise of one of his friends to visit her, after he was gone.

He spoke with delight of the Lord's Prayer, and of adding words of our own to it, and said, "I think that's enough." After some conversation on this subject, he said, lying down in the bed for a moment, and clasping his hands, and raising his eyes, "For a poor little ignorant child who knows hardly anything, I think this is quite sufficient: 'Lord, look down upon a little child'—then pausing a moment—'Lord, visit a little child'—and again, pausing rather longer—'Lord, visit a little child, and give me a new heart.'"

During one of my visits, he called me to his side, and said, with much sweetness of voice and a heavenly expression, "There is a little hymn," (showing the little book I had given him,)

'I'll never, no never, no never forsake.'

This was at a time when his distress was so great, that it was difficult for him to speak.

At another time he wished me to read the hymn,

'How firm a foundation, ye saints of the Lord.'

He seemed to love to *dwell* upon the last verse as though it gave him strength and comfort.

His last words to me were, I believe, a request to visit his mother, and to pray for him. I saw him the day before his death. He was in great distress, but very patient.

A short time before his death, Mr. Edwards, a miniature painter, prepared a sketch of Nathan's countenance, as he was sitting on the bed-side, in one of his most usual attitudes,[43] which has since been engraved, and is prefixed to this Memoir.[44]

After the sketch was taken, he turned to Mr. Edwards, and said, "Won't you let me see it?"

As he looked over the penciling he said to his mother, "Mamma, there's my dent in my chin."

When he saw Mr. Edwards about to go, and that the drawing was not to be left behind, he said anxiously,

"Ain't you going to leave it here for my mother?"

Some one replied, "No, not this one, but your mother shall have one later."

When they had gone, said Nathan to his mother, "Mamma, after I'm gone, you'll have it to look at, and how much it will look like me, there's my dent in my chin."

The affectionate interest which he took in his parents' welfare and happiness after he should be gone was truly affecting. His father had attended a Universalist meeting on the

---

[43] "Attitudes" is used to focus on the *physical position* of his body, not his emotional state, as is customary in the modern day.

[44] This is now found on the cover of this new edition.

Sabbath, and was rather inclined to believe that the sentiments of that denomination were taught in the Bible. Nathan often conversed with his father on this subject, and always in so filial and affectionate a manner that the parent who loved his son so much, could not but love him more.

One day, while speaking on the subject of being "born again" and of the necessity of repenting and believing in the Lord Jesus Christ, in order to be saved, his father said to Nathan that he never expected to be any better prepared to die than he was then.

It seemed to fill Nathan with grief; he could hardly restrain his tears. But after an evident struggle with his feelings, he said, in a tone of voice which expressed more than pen can describe,

"O, papa, I'm afraid you can't go to heaven as you are now."

A short time before he died, the following conversation took place between Nathan and his father. It was related to me by Mr. Dickerman, the evening after the funeral.

Nathan was lying on his pillow, and his father was standing at the fire. The room was still, and all had been for a few moments silent.

Nathan spoke with a sweet voice, and said, "Papa, will you come here?"

His father was immediately at his bedside.

"Now, papa," said the affectionate little son, "if you will leave the Universalist meeting and go to Dr. Jenks's, you may say anything to me, and do anything to me that you please, and I'll give you all I've got."[45]

His father replied, "Why, I have got no pew, Nathan."[46]

---

[45] His parents had been accustomed to give him pieces of money occasionally; and friends who visited him often put something into his hand. And as his parents had not known him, for a long time, to spend any of his money without their consent and approbation, he had accumulated, by carefully preserving all that he had received, which became quite a little stock.

[46] At that time a family had to either purchase a pew or have someone give them a pew for the family to sit together in the church.

"Well, papa," said he, "that needn't hinder you; I will speak to some one who comes in, and get you a seat."

Not long after this, Mr. B who had been one of Nathan's best and earliest friends, and was one of Dr. Jenks's members, came in. Nathan accosted him immediately on the subject which was so near his heart.

"Mr. B., papa says he would go to Dr. Jenks's church if he had a pew."

Mr. B. offered to remove that objection.

The next day Mr. H., another gentleman of Nathan's early acquaintance, and who had endeared himself to him by very many attentions, called to see him.

Nathan made nearly the same address to Mr. H.

Mr. H. replied, "Well, my dear, I have two pews, and shall be very happy to have your papa and mamma and sisters occupy either of them."

When his father came home that night, the first thing Nathan had to say was,

"Papa, Mr. H. says you may have *his* pew and welcome."

"But," replied the father, "I shouldn't go so, I should choose to take a pew *myself*."

"Well," said Nathan, *"don't* let that prevent you; you can pay for it if you have a mind to."

When the father told me the story, he remarked, "I can never forget what that affectionate little boy said, as long as I have my being."

One Sabbath morning, a week or fortnight before his death, I called just as the family had gone to the church meeting. Nathan said, as soon as I entered, with a tone of voice that told how much pleasure it gave him,

"O, Mr. Abbott, papa has gone to Dr. Jenks's, and Rebecca and Maria."

I was once talking with him about the chief priests and scribes who wished to have the Savior crucified. It was after he had heard the account of the crucifixion read. I said that the priests in those days were the ministers. That they pretended to be very good men, but were often very wicked. And so it was now. Some persons who professed to be Christians, and even some ministers of the Gospel, it was to be feared, were very wicked men.

This was said without intending any individual or any denomination. But Nathan looked up to me with a countenance showing that he was grieved at the thought.

"Yes sir, Mr._____," naming a Universalist minister.

And once, in conversation, he said of those who believed those doctrines, "They don't believe the Bible. I don't see how they *can* believe so."

And at another, after having said about the same thing, he added, "When I think of them, it seems as though I could cry."

The affection he manifested towards his mother was equally strong. She was, of course, his constant companion, while his father must necessarily have been absent most of the day. But his tender attachment to them both, as manifested on many occasions, has drawn tears from the eyes of strangers, who witnessed the proofs of his affection. And his parents will never forget the fond love of their son, now that he has gone, nor can they soon cease to remember the earnest and affectionate words which he spoke while he was yet present with them.

During his sickness he was once rocking in his mother's arms at a late hour in the evening. The rest of the family had retired, and they were left alone, everything around them being as still and quiet as slumber. Nathan had been looking very thoughtfully, into the dying embers, for some time, and at length looked up to his mother and said,

"Mamma, I've been thinking I don't know how I can leave you, but God will take care of you, if you will put your trust in him."

At another time, when they were sitting together, he said in a most affectionate manner, "Mamma, do you love your Savior?"

"Yes," Nathan, she replied, "I hope I do." He was silent a moment, and then added,

95

"Now, mamma, do you say so just to please me, or do you feel it in your heart? You know

> 'God does not care for what we say,
> unless we *feel* it too.'

One pleasant afternoon when they were left free from company, he said, "Now, Mamma, the folks are gone out, and it's all still, I want you to pray with me once;—I *want* to *hear* you that I may know you can pray, before I die."

About a month before he died, he was talking with his mother, about her being left alone, when he was gone. And as he spoke of the many friends who had called during his sickness, he said, "Oh, Mamma, they *will* come and see *you,* when I'm gone, —I would ask them, if I thought they wouldn't."

He paused a moment, and then added, "Well, Mamma, if they don't come, you can read your Bible, and think of me, and that will give you comfort."

The day before he died, he said to her,

"Mamma, do you *think* you have an interest in Christ?"[47] She replied faintly, "I'm afraid not."

"O, don't say *so*," said he, bursting into tears; "how happy I would feel if I knew you did."

Nathan's willingness to die and the ground of that willingness appear beautifully in the following account which a lady gives of one of her visits.

I called very soon after a physician had left him; some one was mentioning in the room, what had been said, that the disease was of such a nature, that he would probably die suddenly. Nathan heard it, and rising up in the bed, clasped his hands together, and repeated the verse,

> 'Jesus can make a dying bed
> Feel soft as downy pillows are:
> While on his breast I lean my head,
> And breathe my life out sweetly there.'

---

[47] This expression, "an interest in Christ", was a popular phrase at that time, likely because of the Puritan book *The Christian's Great Interest* by William Guthrie.

And after sitting a few moments in silence, he added another,

> 'Jesus, my God, I know his name,
> His name is all my trust;
> Nor will he put my soul to shame,
> Nor let my hope be lost.'

"Isn't that a good hope, mamma?"

A gentleman once called to see Nathan, and stepping up lightly to his door, found it ajar, and heard some one singing in a low, sweet voice, the first verse above. On entering the room, he found it was Nathan, who was there left alone.

Very early one morning, before he arose, his mother heard him whispering to himself, "Precious Savior, let me die."

She said to him, "Why do you say so, Nathan?"

He answered, "O, mamma, I long to be gone."

On one occasion, Mrs. Dickerman awoke in the night, and missed Nathan from her side. She discovered that he was sitting up in the bed, and said to him, "You had better lie down, Nathan. I'm afraid you will take cold."

He replied, "Don't mamma,—let me sit a little,—how precious Christ is to me."

Once in the middle of the night, his mother heard him talking, as she supposed, to himself, in his sleep. She said, in order to awake him, "What are you talking about, Nathan?"

"Don't, mamma," said he, "I'm trying to pray."

After a very distressing day he said, "Mamma, I feel too tired to *pray*,—won't it do to *think* it?" and then repeated, with earnest emphasis, "Do *you think* it will do, mamma?"

Two ladies were present, at a time when he was in very great bodily distress. One of them said to him,

"Don't you sometimes want to die, and go away from this world, ("Yes," he interposed) and be relieved from your sufferings?" "*No*," he then said, and as she finished her remark, "Not because of my sufferings,—I would like to be with my Savior."

At one time his physician thought he was troubled at the thought of dying; and that possibly he might be thinking, a great portion of his time, about death. He accordingly asked him, in order to ascertain the fact, what was the first thing he thought about in the morning. He replied, "Jesus Christ."

One morning, a gentleman, Mr. L, one of Nathan's particular friends, was with him. He was about to leave the city, and was going to a neighboring town, where Mr. Abbott, another of his friends, had gone. Mrs. Dickerman asked Nathan if he had any message to send to Mr. Abbott—.

"O, yes," he replied, "tell him I'm very happy—my Savior is precious—and if we don't meet on earth again I hope we shall meet in heaven."

As Nathan gave his message, to Mr. L, his father was much affected, shed tears, and left the room.

Nathan noticed it, and said to his mother, "Mamma, do you think papa thinks I shall ever get well?"

"I don't know, dear," she answered.

"I'm afraid he don't," said he, "for he cried when I told Mr. L," &c.

There was one trait in his character, which, at his early age, was truly as remarkable, as it is rare; *real humility*. His feelings were often wounded by the injudicious conversation which was too often held in his presence. Kind friends indulged in, perhaps, what were well-meant, but sadly ill-judged remarks in his presence. And it is most deeply to be regretted that parents and friends so often, inconsiderately no doubt, speak before children, in praise of their persons, in a manner that inevitably fosters vanity, which injures their usefulness and happiness as long as they live.

Nathan's ear was often greeted with, "Beautiful boy!" "Remarkable boy!" "What a fine countenance!" "Certainly the most wonderful case I ever heard of, and the half had not been told me!"

After people have retired, and left such remarks as those behind them for Nathan to think of, he has many a time, to his mother, said something like this:

"Mamma, I wish people wouldn't talk so. What *makes* them think so? I don't think so." "I don't like to hear people say so."

"What makes people say so?" "Mamma, I'm afraid people think I'm better than I am."

"I feel *distressed*," his mother distinctly remembers that he once said, "for fear people should think I'm better than what I am."

Jan. 1, 1830. The day before he died, as his father and mother were in the room, he asked them to bring his little box. He took out his penknife and said to his father,

"Papa I give *you* my knife,—keep it to remember me by."

And to his mother, he said, "Mamma, I give *you* my *Saint's Rest*, and keep it to remember me by."

When his parents were making inquiry for a suitable school for his younger sister, he requested that she might be sent to his former school mistress,—"because," said he, "she is pious, and has prayers in her school."

He also expressed a strong desire to see his elder sister's teacher, for he said, "I want to have her *talk* with Maria,—I'm afraid she does not think enough about her Savior."

He one day received a visit from a pious little girl, and after she had gone away, he said, "O Maria, if I only knew that *you* loved the Savior."

He also particularly desired that they might both continue at the Sabbath School where he had attended.

During the day, Dr. F. came in, and Nathan called him to his bed, and said,

"Won't you please to sit down by the side of me?"

"Doctor F." he then said, in a low tone, "How long do you think I can stand it?" Dr. F. replied, "It is uncertain."

Nathan then asked, "Do you think my lungs are affected?"

The doctor replied, with astonishment that so young a child should ask this question so understandingly. Nathan immediately continued,

"Dr. F., after I am gone, I want you to examine me." He had requested this of Dr. F. once about a month before.

He was one day speaking to his mother on this subject, and she made some remarks, expressing those feelings that are almost instinctive in everybody.

"But, mamma," he replied, "It won't hurt my body any after I am gone, and I want folks to know how much I have suffered."

Today he was very sick indeed. In the afternoon his mother said to him, "Nathan, it is New Year's Day."

"Well mamma," he replied, "I don't expect to see another New Year *here*, but I expect I shall be where it will be always New Year."

At a late hour in the evening of today, he was suddenly taken with a very ill turn. The difficulty of breathing was so great, that at times he seemed to be fetching his last gasp. In the extremity of distress he almost fainted away. He said to his mother, who was anxiously noticing what she supposed to be the last symptoms of his disease,

"Mamma, I'm going."

She raised his body from the pillow, but it seemed indeed for a little time, as if the spirit had left its earthly tabernacle. He, however, soon revived, and said again, in a faint, but pleasant, tone of voice,

"Mamma, I'm going."

Just as the clock struck twelve he said, "Mamma you must lay down aside of me, or you know I can't go to sleep."

It was only a few minutes afterwards that he whispered, as though he was suffering,

"What time are you going to get up, mamma?"

"Now, if you wish, Nathan. Do you want anything? Would you like some drink?" He replied, "O mamma, I'm going."

As they rubbed him with camphor, in order to revive him, he said, "That won't do me any good, I'm going."

They also bathed his feet in warm water, for the same purpose, but he said,

"That won't do me any good! I'm going, I'm going, mamma."

Mrs. Dickerman then said to him, "Had I better call your father?"

"Yes," he said, "call papa."

His father came immediately, and his mother said to him, "Mr. Dickerman, I should like to have you go for the doctor. If *there is* any alteration, I should like to know it."

Nathan said, "There is, mamma."

They had succeeded in reviving him a little from his faintness, but his breathing was so difficult and labored, that they supposed his little remaining strength could not sustain the struggle. They offered him some little cordial to taste, but he declined it, saying,

"*Nothing,* will do me any good, I'm going." At this time he kept his eye fastened upon his mother, and said to her,

"Mamma are you mourning?"

Wherever she went, either around the room, or into the closet, to get anything, his eye followed her.

She said to him, "What do you watch mamma so for, Nathan?"

"'Because I like to, mamma," he replied. He repeated the question, "Mamma, are you mourning?"

"No dear," she answered.

But as she stood over him watching the last struggles of her dying son, he saw the tear upon her cheek. He looked at her tenderly, and raising his hand, gently wiped it away, shaking his head.

The severity of his pain gradually subsided, until near morning, and he seemed comparatively easy and cheerful.

As day began to dawn, his mother said,—"What makes you smile so Nathan?"

"So easy, and so happy mamma," he replied.

The morning Nathan died; Maria came into the room, very early. She understood from some one that he was dying. She came to Mrs. Dickerman and began to cry. Nathan said,

"What are you crying for, Maria?"

She made him no answer.

He then said, "Mamma, what is Maria crying for?"

"She is afraid you are dying."

He said, "*Don't* cry, Maria, *don't* cry," then says to me, "*You* are crying, mamma."

"No, Nathan."

He then said, "Don't any of you cry for me,"—then laid his head down upon the pillow, and fell asleep. This was very early.

About 6 o'clock, he overheard Mrs. Dickerman saying, "I wish Mr. B, or some one, would come in. Nathan then spoke and said, "Send for him, mamma."

When Mr. B. came, Nathan gave him a little hymn book, and said,

"I want you to read it to the Sabbath School children:" and asked, "Are there any children who have become pious?"

Mr. B. replied, "I believe there are two or three."

He then laid his head on the pillow, and resting a moment, raised it again, and looking at Mr. B, said, with a smile, "That pleases me. Tell, tell them they must all love the Savior, and pray to him; if not, when they come to die, it will be dreadful, very dreadful."

He then said to Mr. B.,

"I wish you would talk with Rebecca about the Savior;" and then added, "Now mind Rebecca, what Mr. B. says."

And while Mr. B. was conversing with his little sister, he said, looking up to his mother,

"Now mamma, hark,——I want to hear."

Afterwards, his little sister Maria was standing about and crying bitterly. Nathan said to her,—"Maria, what *do* you cry so for? Mamma, what *makes* Maria, cry so? Don't cry for me."

About nine o'clock, his two little sisters left him to go to school. His last words to them as they went out, were,

"Don't weep for me."

In the course of the morning, his mother had occasion, sometimes to go out of the room. Nathan said to her once,

"Mamma don't you be gone long."

"Why, Nathan?" she asked.

He replied, "I'm afraid I shall die, while you are out of the room,—and I shall want to say something to you."

When Dr. Jenks arrived, his mother whispered to him, "Dr. Jenks has come." He started up from his pillow and said, confusedly, "Where, mamma?"

Dr. Jenks informed him, with tenderness and caution that he would not probably live many hours. Nathan soon after said,

"Dr. Jenks, will you please to go to prayer with me?"

"What shall I pray for?" said the minister.

"That I may be prepared to go," Nathan replied.

During the prayer, he lay with his face almost concealed in the pillow; and after it, said,

"Mamma, will you take me up? I should like to say something to Dr. Jenks."

As she held him in her arms, Dr. Jenks asked him, how long he thought he should continue.

He replied in the words of his physician, "It's uncertain."

"Well, my dear boy," said Dr. Jenks, "I will tell you what I think.—It is our communion Sabbath tomorrow; and I think you will not live to see another Sabbath on earth."

After a moment's pause, he asked the question, "Does this give you any alarm?"

"O no, sir," Nathan replied strongly.

Some one repeated in his hearing, the remark of Dr. F that he would probably drop away instantly; perhaps in two seconds, he might be gone.

Nathan repeated after him, with animation, *Two seconds,* —only think mamma, how quick I shall be with my Savior."

He looked again to his mother who he saw was much affected, and said with stronger emphasis than before, "Mamma, *are you* mourning, you *mustn't* mourn."

About an hour before he died, Mrs. R came in, and while conversing with him, asked if he had not some word to send to her little children, he replied,

"I would like to, but I don't feel able."

Soon after this, Mrs. Dickerman was left a few moments alone with him. She placed him sitting on the bedside; a little stool supported his feet while he rested his arms upon the top of a chair. A pillow was laid lengthwise across its top. His left hand held his elbow, and both rested on the pillow, while he sustained his head by leaning his temple on his right hand.

He said, "Mamma will you please to open the shutters; I can't see." His mother asked, "Can't you see me?"

He answered, "Not very well."

Presently Mrs. H and Miss S came in. One of them asked, "Nathan do you think you shall live through the day?"

He answered, "It's uncertain."

He afterwards said to one of the ladies,

"Won't you stop a little while?" And again,

"Won't you help my mother tomorrow?"

About eleven o'clock, a very distressed turn came upon him. His mother put a piece of orange to his mouth, and in receiving it some of the juice dropped upon the pillow. He said,

"There mamma, I've stained your pillow."

Mrs. H was now supporting his head with one hand, and endeavoring to render his posture as easy as possible by applying the other to his back, as a support.

He said faintly, "Too hard," and then "That's right."

A change was soon noticed in his appearance. He became less restless, and his head was more heavy in her hand. Mrs. H supposing that his hour was come, requested Mrs. Dickerman to take her place. In making the exchange, and receiving his head into her hand, his mother perceived the change and asked,

"Do you know me Nathan?"

"Yes mamma," he said with one of his sweetest smiles. He then endeavored to say something, but his speech was so feeble and broken that they could not understand it.

Mrs. Dickerman then repeated her question,

"Do you know me, Nathan?"

He bowed assent with the same happy expression of countenance as before. She added, "Can you kiss mamma?"

"I would mamma, but"_____. He coughed—threw his head back,—the chair and cricket fell over on the floor,—he reclined gently on the pillow behind him; his eyes were closed; his spirit was with his Savior.

His father soon returned. On opening the door of the room, and seeing his weeping wife and daughters, he fainted entirely away, and fell prostrate on the floor.

A letter written by a lady, a few moments after Nathan expired, begins as follows,—

"I write from the 'privileged' chamber of little Nathan,— quite on the verge of heaven.

"The dear departed is still lying in his sick gown, and at this instant, his father is bedewing his face with tears, and kissing his much loved son."

His funeral was attended the Monday following, at Braintree, where his grandparents reside. A numerous collection of Sabbath School children and friends assembled at the meeting-house, and after prayer by the Rev. Mr. Perkins, an address was delivered by Rev. Mr. Storrs.—A discourse was expected from Rev. Dr. Jenks, but he was detained at home by severe sickness in his own family.

The remains of little Nathan now slumber in the village churchyard of Weymouth, Massachusetts.

POSTSCRIPT TO THE READER

Dear reader, you have now completed this moving account of a young boy's testimony of Christ's sustaining grace in the midst of great suffering. How did this book find you when you first picked it up? How does it find you *now*? Has the Lord spoken to *your* heart?

The publisher has sent forth this book with the prayerful hope that it will be useful in leading many little ones to God. In the words of young Nathan, *"Love the Savior, and pray to him, and read the Bible and DO NOT PUT IT OFF."*

SPECIAL RECOMMEDATIONS
From His Own Time

Pierce & Parker have recently published a new edition of the MEMOIR OF NATHAN W. DICKERMAN, who died at Boston, Jan. 2, 1830, in the eighth year of his age

These Memoirs have been favored with numerous highly commendatory notices, in many of the most respectable periodicals and journals of the country, which are too lengthy to be republished here. The Publishers, however submit from clergymen of different denominations the following recommendations:

"The subscriber has perused with much interest a *Memoir of Nathan W. Dickerman.* He does not hesitate to express the opinion that its circulation is peculiarly calculated to promote the cause of Religion."

Alonzo Porter, Rector of St. Paul's Church, Boston

"I have perused the *Memoir of Nathan W. Dickerman* as far as my pressing avocations at this time would permit. To say that I am pleased with the Book would not be saying what I feel. I would thank the *God of all grace,* for so bright an example of piety among *us,* and at so early an age. The case of *Nathan* is another proof of the capacity and discriminating power of the infant mind, of the power of divine grace, and of the importance of early religious instruction. While it may be regarded as another argument in favor of the institution of Sabbath Schools, it should afford encouragement to the teachers in them to go on in their work, seeing they may expect the fruit of their labors so soon."

T. Merritt, the Methodist Episcopal Church, Boston

"It having been suggested, that a wider circulation of the *Memoir of Nathan W. Dickerman* would be effected if some further testimonial to its perfect credibility, and recommendations of the work itself, were given by persons acquainted with the author and subject: we, the undersigned, having been conversant with both, do cordially recommend the Memoir, as a plain statement of the wonder-working grace of God, which has been manifested among ourselves. The work in our opinion is peculiarly interesting, and deserves the diligent perusal of the rising generation especially, and an extensive circulation through the community."

> Wm. Jenks, Pastor of Green St. Church
> B.B. Wisner, Pastor of Old South Church
> Warren Fay, Charlestown
> J. Greenleaf, Pastor of Bethel Church
> J.W. Fairchild, Pastor of Church at South Boston
> G.W. Bladgen, Pastor of Salem St. Church
> A. Sheldon, City Missionary

Boston, July 6, 1831

"I had not the pleasure of an acquaintance with the interesting little boy of whom the Memoir is written, but am much pleased with it from the interest my own family and the Sabbath School children have taken in it. I cheerfully recommend it to the public, as being well calculated to be useful to the rising generation."

> Edward T. Taylor, of the Methodist Episcopal Church

Other Related SGCB Titles

In addition to *Early Piety Illustrated* Solid Ground Christian Books is honored to offer a full dozen other uncovered treasure for children and young people.

The Child's Book on the Fall by Thomas H. Gallaudet is a simple and practical exposition of the Fall of man into sin, and his only hope of salvation.

The Child's Book on the Soul by Thomas H. Gallaudet, the apostle to the deaf in America, is a remarkable book introducing little children to the reality and value of their immortal soul. No other book like it!

The Child at Home by John S.C. Abbott is the sequel to his popular book *The Mother at Home*. A must read for children and their parents.

My Brother's Keeper: *Letters to a Younger Brother* by J.W. Alexander contains the actual letters Alexander sent to his ten year old brother.

The Scripture Guide by J.W. Alexander is filled with page after page of information on getting the most from our Bibles. Invaluable!

Feed My Lambs: *Lectures to Children* by John Todd is drawn from actual sermons preached in Philadelphia, PA and Pittsfield, MA to the children of the church, one Sunday each month. A pure gold-mine of instruction.

Heroes of the Reformation by Richard Newton is a unique volume that introduces children and young people to the leading figures and incidents of the Reformation. He was called by Spurgeon, *"The Prince of preachers to the young."*

Heroes of the Early Church by Richard Newton is the sequel to the above-named volume. The very last book Newton wrote introduces all the leading figures of the early church with lessons to be learned from each figure.

The King's Highway: *Ten Commandments to the Young* by Richard Newton is a volume of Newton's sermons to children. Highly recommended!

The Life of Jesus Christ for the Young by Richard Newton is a double volume set that traces the Gospel from Genesis 3:15 to the Ascension of our Lord and the outpouring of His Spirit on the Day of Pentecost. Excellent!

The Young Lady's Guide by Harvey Newcomb will speak directly to the heart of the young women who desire to serve Christ with all their being.

The Chief End of Man by John Hall is an exposition and application of the first question of the Westminster Shorter Catechism. It is intended to be read by both Sunday School children and their teachers. Full of rich illustrations.

Other Solid Ground Titles